Gay a[...]
Tourism: The Essential Guide for Marketing

To Rebecca —
A woman with vision, creativity &
foresight — congratulations & thank
you —
Jeff

Gay and Lesbian Tourism: The Essential Guide for Marketing

Jeff Guaracino

AMSTERDAM • BOSTON • HEIDELBERG • LONDON • NEW YORK • OXFORD
PARIS • SAN DIEGO • SAN FRANCISCO • SINGAPORE • SYDNEY • TOKYO
Butterworth-Heinemann is an imprint of Elsevier

Butterworth-Heinemann is an imprint of Elsevier
Linacre House, Jordan Hill, Oxford OX2 8DP, UK
30 Corporate Drive, Suite 400, Burlington, MA 01803, USA

First edition 2007

British Library Cataloguing in Publication Data
A catalogue record for this book is available from the British Library

Library of Congress Cataloging-in-Publication Data
A catalog record for this book is available from the Library of Congress

ISBN: 978-0-7506-8232-9

For information on all Butterworth-Heinemann publications
visit our web site at books.elsevier.com

Printed and bound in Great Britain
07 08 09 10   10 9 8 7 6 5 4 3 2 1

This book is dedicated to my mother, Lucille Guaracino,
who taught me to love God, and to my partner,
Dr. Brian Little, who taught me the meaning of love
and loving life

Author Biography

 Jeff Guaracino is vice president of communications for the Greater Philadelphia Tourism Marketing Corporation (GPTMC). The Philadelphia Get Your History Straight and Your Nightlife Gay®, the ground-breaking gay tourism campaign, has won top awards in the public relations, advertising and travel industries. The Philadelphia campaign has been widely recognized as an innovative model that has proven its effectiveness in generating business and in building the image of the destination. Guaracino also oversees the Hispanic, African-American, and Canadian communication programs.

Previously, Guaracino served as director of communications for the Franklin Institute, (Philadelphia's premier science museum) and prior to that, was communications associate CBS, Inc. and public relations manager at the AIDS Coalition of Southern New Jersey. Active in the community, he serves as a marketing and public relations consultant to a number of regional organizations where he specializes in crisis communications and marketing. Formerly served on the board of the William Way GLBT Community Center. He is also a member of the National Lesbian and Gay Journalists Association and served on the host committee for the national convention in September 2002. Guaracino is a graduate of Rowan University and has studied at Temple University. He resides in Philadelphia, Pennsylvania.

Contents

Foreword

Kimpton Hotels and Restaurants has always been supportive of the lesbian, gay, bisexual and transgender (LGBT) community. It only makes sense. As a company specializing in hospitality, our first priority will always be serving all people with dignity and respect.

Kimpton's gay and lesbian outreach program grew out of the company's diversity program. The company was founded in San Francisco in the early 1980's and we have always valued diversity in the workplace. While in the early years of the company, we did not have a recognized LGBT outreach program, the gay and lesbian community certainly recognized us. We were viewed as a perfect fit for the community, offering hotels known for their hip and unique environments, innovative guest programs, and personnel policies that established Kimpton on the leading edge of workplace equality. It was our corporate values that established our presence within the gay and lesbian community first.

Kimpton's relationship with the gay and lesbian community is based on sound business practices. We invest in marketing programs when we believe we will see a return on our investment. Research has firmly established that the gay and lesbian community travels frequently, is more brand loyal, and is more likely to stay in upscale hotels. But even an established gay-friendly company like Kimpton needed to learn the best practices of serving the LGBT community.

Unfortunately, we did not have a book like *Gay and Lesbian Tourism: The Essential Guide for Marketing* to help us. Instead we relied on our gay and lesbian employees for input as well as information from organizations like HRC and Out & Equal. First, we established gay-friendly work environments and personnel practices. While we had always given back to the community, we next looked at organizing our commitment with our annual Red Ribbon Campaign for HIV/AIDS charities across the country. Then we researched and implemented appropriate marketing and sales tracking strategies. Finally, we empowered our LGBT employees and guests to spread the word about Kimpton's commitment to the gay and lesbian community.

In 2006, we were able to track well over five million dollars in business from the gay and lesbian community, and we know that number is much higher if you count community members that have not yet identified themselves through our customer loyalty programs.

Of course none of this can be effective if your company is not authentic. Being gay-friendly is not just about throwing a rainbow flag on your brochures and programs. For Kimpton, being gay-friendly is about being true to our core corporate beliefs – of treating all of our internal and external customers with dignity and respect. We are thrilled that the LGBT market has fallen in love with Kimpton – and plan to continue to build the program. Not only is it the right thing to do – it makes sound business sense.

We are proud to include our success as a case study in this publication and we applaud Jeff Guaracino and his efforts to provide companies new to the LGBT market with a guide to market success.

Niki Leondakis
Chief Operating Officer
Kimpton Hotels & Restaurants

Michael Depatie
CEO & President
Kimpton Hotels & Restaurants

Acknowledgements

Thank you to everyone at Elsevier publishing, especially Jane MacDonald, who took a chance on a first-time author, and to the entire production, editing, sales and marketing team for making this book possible. You have made this book a reality.

Thank you to everyone who has changed my professional and personal life, especially Brian Little, Joanne Calabria, Bruce Yelk, Brian Goldthrope, Nina Zucker, Lynda Bramble, Kevin Hanaway, Sue and Brandon Hamilton, Shawn C. and Michelle Waters, Bruce and Michelle Shannon and Mark Segal. My family Jerry, Kim, Taylor, Luke, Travis, Marlene and Dominick Matteo, Theresa and William Sauer, Mary and Dennis Guaracino and their entire families and the Littles. My friends Jessica and George, John and Ricky, Peggy, Joe and Norris, Andrea and Mark, Anthony and Franco, Jonathan (a.k.a Miss Kitty) and Matthew, Jeff and Stan, Kevin and Drew, Marcia and Maria, Old City Ironworks Crew, Tony, Laura, Stu and Jennifer, Dan and Holly, Mike, Owen, Bill and Alejandra and Penelope, Mark, Dan, Charlie, DJ and Christine, and everyone who I wish I could have included but you know who you are. Sorry that I have not been around much. Being this gay takes a lot of time and I love you. I can never thank you enough for loving me, nurturing me and accepting me.

My teachers and pioneers in gay travel who have become my friends, Jeff Marsh, Ed Salvato, Matt Link, Michael Luongo, Gregg Kaminsky, Matt Farber, Helene Fortier, Yves Pelliter, Richard Grey, Mark Tewksbury, Eric Hegedus, Steven K. Smith, Serge Gojkovich, R. Bruce McDonald, Jill Pentrack, Martina Navratilova, Kelli and Rosie O'Donnell, Wes Combs, George Carrancho, Betty Young, Andrew Freeman, Michael Doughman, Ben Finzel, Todd Evans, J.R. Pratts, Mike Wood, Don Tuthill, Matt Skallerud, Judy Wieder, Francine Mason, Justin Garrett, George Neary, Tom Roth and his team Jerry, Glenn and David and all my friends who attend the International Gay and Lesbian Tourism Conference. Mike Wilke from the Commercial Closet and Bob Wietck from Wietck-Combs, thank you for your invaluable contributions to this book. I am eternally grateful. You rock!

Thank you to the gay pioneers who fought for our civil rights. It is on your shoulders the next generation stands.

The fabulous board and incredible staff at the Greater Philadelphia Tourism Marketing Corporation, led by the incomparable Meryl, Sharon, Paula, Deborah, Andy, Patricia, Angela, Mike, Jim, Kristen, Linda, Libby, Sabrina, Sheila, Vicky, Leha, John, Bruce, Joyce, Cathy, Cara, Jayson Donna, Chris, Caroline, Anthony, Morgan, Ayele, Matthew, Veronica, Christian, James, Tendai, Keith, Rachel, Anne, Jeffrey, Maria, Suzanne, Roz, Luz, Norman, Susan and everyone that I didn't have room to include, I thank you for everything.

I would like to especially acknowledge Meryl Levitz, who everyday inspires the best and demands excellence. Thank you for your trust in my abilities and for knowing just the right questions to ask. Your long support of the gay community has helped strengthen a community. We've have always needed advocates like you. You have helped to change the world, you have transformed Philadelphia and you have changed my life. I love you back and I've got your back!

Everyone at the National Lesbian and Gay Journalists Association especially Pam Strother, Eric Hegedus, Court Passant, Michael McCarthy, Gail Shister, Stuart Elliott and my pals who I see just once a year at the annual NLGJA convention. You know who you are and thank you. My friends at Enterprise Rent-A-Car, Southwest Airlines and *Where* Magazine.

Everyone at The Philadelphia Gay Tourism Caucus including Tami Sortman, Malcolm Lazin, Bruce Yelk, Brian Weaver, Tony Geisweite, Mel Heitfitz, Dave Jefferys, Laura Burkthardt, the CVBs of Southeastern Pennsylvania, and the Philadelphia GLBT community. Everyone at Comcast Spotlight especially Jim Gallagher, Ann Letizi, Tom Wise and all my friends who always supported GPTMC and me. You are the stars of the Philadelphia show.

Thank you Governor Rendell, Mickey Rowley, Richard Bonds and the entire staff at the Pennsylvania Tourism Office, Mayor John Street, Stephanie Naidoff and the staff at the Commerce Department, Philadelphia City Council, the Pennsylvania legislature including Senator Fumo and Representative Roebuck for supporting the GLBT community and the gay tourism marketing effort. You are champions. I would also like to thank everyone who contributed to this book through their time, talents and perspective.

Finally, I would like to acknowledge myself. I had no idea what I was getting into! I had no experience in writing a book but I did it. I made a bet with myself, write a book or get a master's degree. Well, I pitched something without fear of failure. I learned how to do it and looked around my vast network of resources to advise me, to inspire me and to educate me. I did the best that I could do. Perhaps, the most valuable lesson that I learned is that I couldn't do it alone. I hope you like it, and remember, *buy this book* for your friends, relatives and business colleagues. I am available for speaking engagements. Email me at www.gayandlesbianmarketing.com

Introduction

Congratulations. You are about to learn about the world of gay and lesbian tourism, a $54 billion industry in the United States, according to Community Marketing Incorporated (CMI). CMI is the leading gay and lesbian marketing researching firm. The Travel Industry of America estimates that 85 percent of gay and lesbians take annual vacations compared to the national average of 64 percent.

This book was written with the travel professional in mind. No matter what segment of the hospitality industry you work in (airlines, hotels, cruise lines) or how big or small your destination, this book will be relevant to you and arm you with practical information. When you are finished reading *Gay and Lesbian Tourism: The Essential Guide for Marketing*, you will be prepared to begin the really hard work of launching a campaign. I hope that this book will entertain as well as enlighten you.

This book is the first of its kind. Never before has there been a how-to book written on gay and lesbian tourism marketing. Never before have the case studies that you will read about ever been published in a book.

This book will serve as a one-stop shop so you can learn the best practices of gay tourism marketing. This book seeks to condense the collective knowledge of the gay tourism industry into a gay tourism marketing 101 format. In it, you will find several case studies written either directly by pioneers in gay travel or by one-on-one interviews. These are the people who have paved the way for the rest of us to follow. They will share with you how they began their gay tourism programs. They work in large and small destinations, as well as hotels and airlines. Finally, my mentors have been featured in the Expert Soapboxes. These are some of the most talented people working in the hospitality industry today. In their own words, they will share with you their advice and expertise in the gay tourism market.

How does gay and lesbian travel fit into the big picture of tourism? That is a great question! "Travel and tourism" is about hospitality. People want to travel to experience new things, to have fun and to take home stories that they can tell their friends and family about.

Travel for the GLBT community is no different. However, there is so much more that comes with it. Consider this: Is every gay traveler out? No. Does every gay traveler want to feel safe and welcomed? Yes. There are subtle ways to welcome people and then there are big, gay, fabulous ways to say, "we are glad that you are here."

Extending your marketing campaign to the GLBT traveler says as much about your product as it does by the act itself. What do I mean? Welcoming gay and lesbian travelers is a signal to other groups of people that you appreciate diversity, value creativity and promote acceptance. Gay tourism marketing speaks volumes about what your travel product is all about.

One of my favorite sayings is, if it were easy everyone would do it! Perfecting the art of gay tourism marketing isn't easy but it can be done. This book is a collection of the knowledge that I have accumulated and has been shared with me by the experts in the field.

Ed Salvato, editor of the *Out Traveler* and director of global travel for Planet Out, recalls that there were just about five destinations in 1998 with active marketing campaigns for the gay and lesbian traveler. In 2006, there were at least 67 destinations and more were on the way. If your company is not welcoming to gay travelers, you better get moving because you are losing lots of money and market share.

Jeff Guaracino (Center) with U.S. Presidents Bill Clinton and George Bush.

Today, despite these advances, gay tourism remains controversial. Slowly, this is changing as more companies and destinations join the gay tourism market but even as late as summer of 2006, St. Petersburg, Florida, had a very public debate about going after the gay traveler. Ironically, at the same time that the community of St. Petersburg argued over gay tourism, Visit Florida, the state's tourism arm, announced that it will increase its marketing efforts to gay travelers.

This is not a book with academic theories but with practical, real-world information. It is my hope that you will be able to breeze through this book while traveling somewhere. The world of gay travel is changing fast, so stay informed. Hang on for what will be a very rewarding endeavor.

I am very interested in your comments on this book. Email me at gayandlesbianmarketing@yahoo.com or by visiting my web site www.gayandlesbianmarketing.com for up-to-date information, research and gay and lesbian travel trends. I am available to speak on gay and lesbian tourism at your company, meeting, event, community gathering or convention.

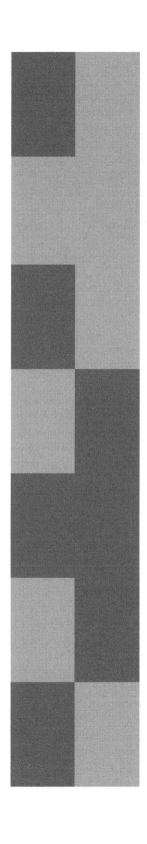

CHAPTER 1

The rise in gay and lesbian tourism, nothing short of historic

Since 2001, cities and countries have come out of the closet as gay-friendly. There are seven reasons for this gay-friendly phenomenon. However, 9/11 is perhaps one of the top reasons.[1–3] In the aftermath of 9/11, gay travelers were the first to come back when the hospitality industry needed the business. At a time when the hospitality industry was saying "Thanks for Traveling" in its marketing campaigns to encourage people to start traveling again, gay travelers never stopped traveling. Really, was it a surprise? Gay travelers must deal with discrimination, hate crimes and hate speech in their everyday lives. Terrorism is not a deterrent to travel for this group of people. At a time when the industry was suffering for business, gay men and lesbians were suddenly the rising stars in travel recovery.

The second reason for the historic rise in gay travel was that in this new millennium gay issues began to dominate news coverage and the public became sensitized to seeing gay people on television and in marketing campaigns. In 1997, Ellen DeGeneres came out and brought a gay person into millions of Americans' homes every week in her sitcom, Ellen. In 2002, America's favorite daytime talk show host Rosie O'Donnell came out of the closet. In November 2003, the United States Supreme Court struck down a Texas sodomy law that punished homosexuals for having deviant sex, meaning that it was no longer a crime to have gay sex in the United States.[4] (Ironically, one of the case studies that you will read later is from Michael Doughman of Dallas, Texas, the heart of conservative United States.) In 2004, the U.S. presidential campaign was won by the Republicans on the issue of gay marriage.[5] In 2005, LOGO, the first national cable television network for the gay, lesbian, bisexual and transgender (GLBT) community, made its debut changing the landscape of national cable television forever by shining a spotlight on the GLBT community 24 hours a day, seven days a week.

The third reason is as simple as this: that gay people wanted to visit new places and they wanted to feel welcomed.[6] Before there were gay tourism marketing campaigns, there were places that were naturally gay-friendly such as perennial favorites, Key West and Provincetown because of their attitude of acceptance of the GLBT community. Both Key West and Provincetown provided an escape from the sometimes conservative lives of travelers that often forced them to be in the closet. These resort towns offered privacy and a vast array of entertainment that engaged the gay sensibilities including drag shows, dancing and nightclubs. Cities like London, New York City and San Francisco have enjoyed nearly a exclusive reputation as gay destinations primarily because of the size of their resident GLBT population and their vast offerings of gay nightlife, arts and culture and jobs. As gay travelers came out, they wanted to see the rest of the world, but they wanted to do it on their own terms and be completely comfortable, which brings us to the fourth reason.

As more and more GLBT people come out of the closet, they are seeking new gay-friendly destinations and gay-friendly travel companies to take them there.[7,8] Gay and lesbian events are great reasons to travel at a particular time of year. The extraordinary rise in gay travel is very closely linked to the growth in events such as Gay Days in Disney World in Florida or the Dinah Shore Golf Classic in Palm Springs. When tens of thousands of gay and lesbian people arrive at a destination all at one time, they are going to get noticed. These events, also known as, "circuit parties" sprang up in cities all over the United States in the 1990s. The annual "White Party" in Miami Beach was the genesis of the circuit party started more than 20 years ago. In cities across the world, gay parties attracting thousands of gay men sprung up including the Blue Ball in Philadelphia, Black & Blue in Montreal and the Winter Party in Miami Beach. Did I mention that all of these events have one thing in common? They all happen during the off-season.

The fifth is the local active GLBT communities and their straight allies as a very strong reason for the historic rise in gay and lesbian travel. Without the dedicated and passionate people living and working in a destination or for a travel supplier, gay-friendly and gay-welcoming travel would not be possible.

The sixth reason is the availability of research from organizations like Community Marketing, Inc., Simmons, Travel Industry of America, Harris Interactive and Wietck–Combs. For the first time, the economic impact of gay travel can be measured and researched.

Finally, it is the extraordinary growth of media outlets to reach the GLBT traveler that makes gay tourism marketing campaigns possible.[9] Today, there are several gay television networks in the United States, millions of websites with content of interest to gay and lesbian travelers, thousands of gay and lesbian newspapers around the world and even mainstream travel television programs that cover gay-friendly travel. In fact, the Travel Channel aired its first hour-long gay travel program in 2006.

Mark Elderkin, Founder of Gay.com, said at a speech at the International Gay and Lesbian Travel Association (IGLTA) convention in 2006 that the evolution of the gay travel market has been 12 years in the making.[10] A brilliant entrepreneur, Mark registered the web domain name, gay.com, well before anyone really understood the power of the Internet. He said that gay travel remains a growth market. He credits the rise in gay travel to GLBT people themselves who are no longer invisible and are an active market force. He's right. The GLBT community is out, vocal and visible. For the very first time, it is possible to mass-market to gay and lesbian travelers. In the past, advertising to the gay and lesbian consumer was first done in underground and dare I say, by then-radical publications.

As gay people are increasingly not hiding in the closet but are out and proud,[11] so are travel suppliers. They are embracing gay travel and are slowly coming out of the closet. Adding to that, the general pubic are gaining more acceptance of GLBT customers, making it more acceptable for companies like Ford to "openly" market to gay customers without alienating other customers.

According to the Commercial Closet, a nonprofit organization that educates advertisers, ad agencies, academics, the media and consumers for more effective and informed references to lesbian, gay, bisexual and transgender people in advertising, over 1000 corporations and 500 ad agencies are represented in the Commercial Closet Ad Library, in categories such as alcohol/spirits, appliances, automotive, beauty, beverages, electronics, fashion, food, footwear, financial services, government, healthcare, media, packaged goods, restaurants, retail, soft drinks, telecommunications, and travel. The Commercial Closet says that American corporations now spend about $232 million annually in gay media and major sponsorships.

Between 2000 and 2004 there was a slow buildup of destinations coming out. However, 2005 and 2006 were pivotal years in gay tourism with a record number of destinations coming out as gay-friendly at the same time perhaps now there are 50 or 60 destinations worldwide with coordinated campaigns.[12] Among them are Finland, Spain, Tahiti and Austria. In 2005, Canada[13] and Boston[14] announced their campaigns followed in 2006 by Visit Florida[15] and Atlanta, Georgia.[16] On May 15, 2006, the Canadian Tourism Commission (CTC) launched its first gay and lesbian advertising campaign by appealing to North American gay couples who were looking to have a same-sex marriage. In August 2006, the South African Gay and Lesbian Travel Alliance (SAGLTA), an organization that represents selected South African gay-friendly guesthouses, bed and breakfasts, hotels and various travel-related products, began its first effort to lure international travelers to South Africa. In October 2006, in Hungary, Budapest's tourism website started a section to gay and lesbian travelers, which was widely reported by United Press International.

By 2006, cities and countries all over the world began to recognize that same-sex couples have the right to share in the same legal rights as straight married couples. Canada, South Africa and the United Kingdom are perhaps the most well-known countries for same-sex marriage rights, but even the most conservative cities in religious countries, such as Mexico City, began adding legal protections for same-sex couples. Once the legal system recognizes a gay and lesbian relationship, it also signals a new market for destinations and for companies.[17] Suddenly, it is okay to market to the GLBT community. Gay marriage ceremonies (or same-sex commitment ceremonies as they are also called) bring in gay dollars even for gay honeymoons. Another halo effect of gay marriage is that once the government says it is legal, the gay and lesbian market can become an official category in a business plan, well for smart businesses anyway.

Make no mistake, gay tourism is changing the world and it will change your company, sometimes in unexpected ways. These are the unexpected outcomes.

1. Positive messages to other groups of people. When you promote your destination, cruise line or travel product as gay-friendly, you are sending a signal to other groups of people that you welcome them too. Essentially, people think that if you welcome the GLBT community, you must welcome African Americans, Hispanics, Asians and others.

2. Positive employee morale. Gay tourism marketing also sends a very positive message to your GLBT employees, who are in or out of the closet, and their straight colleagues.

3. Positive image building. Gay stereotypes also play a positive role in the minds of your customers. The stereotype is that gay and lesbian people only travel to places that are exciting and culturally rich. Gay travelers most always seek out a place with a great nightlife and lots of things to do. People believe that gay travelers oftentimes discover the next great place, well before other travelers. Gays are the trendsetters. The sterotype may or may not be true, but it certainly works to your advantage.

What types of trips are gay and lesbians taking? Everything from weekend getaways and city breaks to food tours or cultural weekends. Outdoor adventure is a huge growth market within the gay community.[18] Gay travelers are going to the traditional gay hot spots like Key West, Florida, Philadelphia, Provincetown, Massachusetts, and Mykonos, Greece. They are also exploring a whole new world of destinations including Vancouver, Canada, Minneapolis, Minnesota, Las Vegas, Nevada, Phoenix, Arizona, Sydney, Australia, Sao Paulo, Brazil, Cape Town, South Africa, Manchester, England and there was even a private charter ship to the South Pole.

What does gay tourism marketing all come down to? Simply this:

> It is the power of the invitation. Before people will come, they must be invited.

"Marketers must not forget that people want to be invited," said Meryl Levitz, president and CEO of the Greater Philadelphia Tourism Marketing Corporation (GPTMC).[19] "People need to be invited and you do that by choosing imagery that they know is for them, placing it in media that is for them and making a promise of what people can expect all the way through the travel experience. For gay and lesbian travelers who aren't sure if they are going to be welcomed for who they are, an invitation is definitely needed."

Case study

American Airlines

George Carrancho and Betty Young[20]
The Rainbow TeAAm

American Airlines, the granddaddy of savvy gay travel marketing, has almost 15 years of experience in the gay travel market. The world's largest airline, American Airlines, serves 250 cities in 40 countries with more than 4000 daily flights operated by American Airlines, American Eagle and the AmericanConnection® airlines. American Airlines is a for-profit company, a subsidiary of the AMR Corporation, and is listed on the New York Stock Exchange.

George and Betty agree on this core principle when it comes to the gay and lesbian market, it has to be a win for the GLBT organization and for American Airlines. American is a for-profit company, which means it has to be good for the bottom line, it has to be returned and it has to be measurable.

"Our sales and marketing efforts reflect the diversity of our customers," said Betty Young. "Gay customers are loyal to us because of frequent flyer program, American's global route and our reputation in many communities."

On October 31, 2006, American Airlines launched AA.com/rainbow, a webpage for GLBT travelers. American Airlines is the only airline to offer one-stop online welcome for gay travelers. The website promises Lowest Fare Guarantee, up to 1000 AAdvantage® mile booking bonus, no booking fees and content specifically of interest to the gay traveler including an e-newsletter with GLBT travel tips, discounts and deals. American Airlines partnered with gay-friendly hotel chain Wyndham Hotels and Resorts, which offered 20 percent discount on hotel reservations made through AA.com/rainbow. In addition, American Airlines sells many of its products on this section of the website including day passes to its Admirals Club and AA Group and Meeting and Travel.

To market the website, GLBT-focused American Airlines advertisements with "gay codes," either the Human Rights Campaign logo or the rainbow were placed on the travel pages of the GLBT community websites. Also, in a brilliant marketing coup on the grassroots level, American Airlines strategically aligned its business with national and local GLBT organizations and negotiated "an official airline" status with the groups. In addition to building the company's image as a gay-friendly airline dedicated to the issues and solutions provided by trusted GLBT organizations, the Rainbow TeAAm sales group also generates business for the airline by marketing to the GLBT organization constituency base the Business ExtrAA program, a travel incentive program.

The Business ExtrAA program generates business and loyalty for American Airlines by having consumers earn frequent flyer miles on their American Airlines account while at the same time earning miles for their favorite GLBT organization that can use those points for free travel, thus saving the organization money. They call it, "effortless philotrophony."

The Business ExtrAA program is a program that is offered to other travelers not just gay travelers. "Why reinvent the wheel," said George. "American Airlines products are great, sometimes we just need to fine tune it so the gay traveler knows that we are speaking directly to them. In the end we are all just travelers."

American Airlines had not always enjoyed a stellar gay-friendly reputation, it had to work at it. Like so many companies, American Airlines realized the importance of being a gay-friendly airline reinforced by one unfortunate incident. In their book, *Business Inside Out*, Robert Witeck and Wesley Combs, recount the story that forever changed American Airlines, an airline that today is the very best example of how a company should be.

> It all started in June 1993 when many GLBT Americans traveled to Washington, D.C. to take part on the march on Washington. Naturally many chose to fly from distant cities... one flight stood out.... Regrettably, a poorly educated and insensitive member of the flight crew recommended that all of the aircraft's (American's) pillows and blankets used by these (gay) travelers be consigned to rubbish or be systemically sanitized.

Today, American Airlines consistently gets 100 percent on the Human Rights Campaign's Corporate Equality Index. It was among the first airlines to add sexual orientation to its nondiscrimination policies. It was also the first airline to add protections for transgender employees. This airline was the first to implement same-sex partnership benefits, the same as it offers to married heterosexual employees. American Airlines also has a strong and active GLBT employee group called GLEAM.

Notes

1. Wyman, Scott, Gay Tourism Sustains South Florida Through Tough Economic Times, *South Florida Sun-Sentinel News*, November 23, 2001.
2. Garrett, Justin, Planet Out Inc., phone interview, November 2006.
3. Roth, Thomas, Community Marketing Inc., *Gay and Lesbian Tourism Profile*, 2003.
4. *Lawrence et al v. Texas*, 539 U.S. 558, 2003.
5. Blumenthal, Sidney, Bush Goes to War with Modernity, *Guardian* (United Kingdom), March 4, 2004.
6. Trucco, Terry, Counting Gay Travelers, *New York Times*, May 16, 2004.
7. Trucco, Terry, Counting Gay Travelers, *New York Times*, May 16, 2004.
8. Roth, Thomas, Community Marketing Inc., *Gay and Lesbian Tourism Profile*, 2003.
9. Hopkins, Jim, Media Offers New Outlets for Gay Audiences, *USA Today*, March 2, 2006.
10. Elderkin, Mark, International Gay and Lesbian Travel Association Convention, Speech, Washington, D.C., May 27, 2006.
11. GL Census Partners (www.glcensus.org) Study-A Syracuse University and OpusComm Group Research Partnership.
12. Trucco, Terry, Counting Gay Travelers, *New York Times*, May 16, 2004.
13. Robin, Laura, Canada Invites Gay Tourists to Get Out and About, *Canwest News Service*, April 23, 2005.
14. Goodison, Donna, 100G Gay Tourism Campaign Launched, *Boston Herald*, July 20, 2005.
15. Clarke, Susan Strother, Visit Florida Set Sights on $50 Billion-a-Year Gay Market, *Orlando Sentinel*, June 12, 2006.
16. Stafford, Leon, Chasing a Rainbow, *Atlanta Journal-Constitution*, October 6, 2006.
17. Salvato, Ed, Planet Out Inc., in-person interview, South Beach, Miami, September 9, 2006.
18. Salvato, Ed, Planet Out Inc., in-person interview, South Beach, Miami, September 9, 2006.
19. Levitz, Meryl, Greater Philadelphia Tourism Marketing Corporation, interview, September 5, 2006.
20. Carrancho, Young, American Airlines, phone interview, November 3, 2006.

Terminology: getting it straight

Welcome to the world of gay and lesbian tourism! Before we begin, it is important that we are on the same page. And to do that, we must first have a mutual understanding of what things mean. Can you define gay? Sure, we all know what gay means but do you know when to use it and when not. What does GLBT stand for? What is the difference between someone who is bisexual and a lesbian? What does it mean to be gay-friendly? What is a gay family? Is there such a thing as lesbian-friendly?

This chapter is designed to set us straight so we can move forward with common understanding, working from the largest concept of what gay travel means down to the individual terminology that you may have heard of but aren't really sure what the word actually means. In this chapter, you will find a glossary of terms to help you better understand and more efficiently communicate with gay and lesbian travelers. You will also learn about the resources, outside of this book, to help you take your gay-friendly tourism campaign to the next step.

Where did gay travel all begin? Hanns Ebensten (1923–2006) is credited as the "inventor of gay travel".[1] His love for travel led him to create the first organized trip for gay men in 1972. In 2004, the IGLTA named him the Pioneer of Gay Travel and honored him with the renaming of their annual citation of excellence as the Hanns Ebensten IGLTA Hall of Fame Award. He survived the German Holocaust and World War II serving in the British Army.

Ebensten said,

> We designed trips to Morocco, to Greece Turkey and Persia. We went to Galapagos Islands, to Easter Island and to Tahiti. All of our trips were travel adventures. Some were more rudimentary than others but that is immaterial. It is the romanticism of travel that is important.

Let's start with the largest concept, gay travel. Gay travel means that you celebrate and value diversity. In the marketing section of this book, we will be talking a lot about the Rainbow Flag and its symbolic power to communicate a gay-friendly and gay-welcoming message. The Rainbow Flag is perhaps the strongest symbol that represents diversity within the gay community.

"The intent of the flag was to answer the pink triangle as the symbol of the gay movement," said Gilbert Baker in a television interview in May 2006.[2] "Until 1978 the gay triangle had been the iconic symbol of the movement."

The Rainbow Flag was designed in 1978 by Gilbert Baker of San Francisco with six stripes representing the six colors of the rainbow as a symbol of gay and lesbian community pride. The colors on the flag – red, orange, yellow, green, blue, and violet – symbolize the diversity within the GLBT community.[3]

Today, the Rainbow Flag is essentially a gay icon or gay code that is most often used in marketing to communicate gay-friendliness. It is essentially the gay-friendly welcome sign or welcome mat.

In a later chapter, you will also learn that gay travelers are spending more than $54 billion a year in travel in the United States alone[4] and the GLBT adult spending power in 2006 was $641 billion.[5]

While we are on the subject of defining words, let's start with the one word I am most often asked about, gay-friendly. What does it mean to be gay-friendly? It really does depend on the travel product that you are selling but simply put,

> Gay-friendly means that you are making an authentic invitation to the GLBT community; that you conduct your business in a manner that embraces people's diversity

making everyone feel welcomed; and that your business policies don't penalize your GLBT customers or employees.

Gay-family travel means that two dads may have children, two moms may have children, or straight parents may have gay children or straight siblings may have gay brothers or sisters. Family-friendly, gay-friendly travel is multigenerational.[6]

What about lesbian-friendly travel? Most women travelers will tell you that safety and security is the number one concern for female travelers across the board. However, when there are two women traveling together, safety and security is even further heightened. Miami based expert travel journalist LoAnn Holden says that in most cases, if you are gay-friendly, lesbians will be comfortable there too.[7] However, for two women checking into a hotel or a cruise ship cabin, they never, ever want to feel as if they are some kind of object of fantasy for men. She warns that lesbians don't want to feel any sense of that creep factor when they travel. You would be surprised at how often two women see or overhear employees making inappropriate comments when seeing two women checking in together, especially if they want one bed.

Increasingly, destinations and suppliers are using the words "gay welcoming" replacing gay-friendly. Simply put gay welcoming means that you acknowledge gay consumers and you would like their business. A good example of gay welcoming may be Atlantic City. While the city lacks a number of the traditional hallmarks of a gay destination such as gay nightclubs and drag shows, Atlantic City does offer casinos, shopping and entertainment that is of interest to gay and to straight people. Atlantic City is putting out the gay-welcome mat.

So what does gay marketing entail? The first question you have to ask yourself is why do you love the gay market? If your only answer is the money, then you have a lot of work to do. It must be more than the money. Tourism marketing extends an invitation. An invitation is extended to someone you know.[8,9] When you know someone, you are familiar with the words and images that are appealing to them. You understand how to deliver that message and the person receiving it knows that you understand their interests. You should love the gay market because you know the gay traveler and you want them to experience what you have to offer because you think they will enjoy it, remember it and tell their friends about it. The second question you should ask is, am I or how do I become gay-friendly? AMEN! By merely asking the question you are already on your way because you are aware that there is a need to learn how to become a gay-friendly business and you understand that this market, like most niche markets, needs a specific invitation. Throughout this book, you will be presented with a number of ways to demonstrate that you are truly offering an authentic invitation for gay people to travel with your company or to your destination.

While we are on the subject of getting things straight, it is important to note that the GLBT community are multicultural travelers. Gay travelers are African American, Caucasian, Hispanic, Canadian, Italian, Irish, Indian and American Indian. For now, gay and lesbian travel usually falls within the multicultural affairs divisions of convention and visitors bureaus, tourism promotion agencies, travel agencies and even in award categories. Perhaps it is time to rethink where GLBT calls home? Some argue that GLBT belongs within the multicultural segments while others strongly believe that the segment should be renamed. It is essential to find an appropriate home for GLBT because only then can this segment be afforded the necessary resources, both financial and educational, to make a long-term impact.

A word of caution, be careful to avoid negative gay sterotypes. Have you heard the terms lipstick lesbian, circuit boy, queen, dyke, homo, leather daddy, pup, granola lesbian, closet case, daddy or twink? If you don't know what these words mean, you should never use them. That said, Gay stereotypes, however, do play a minor role within gay tourism marketing, which we will get to later on. At the same time, it is important to be aware of positive gay stereotypes. Not every gay person is a DINK (double income, no kids). There are plenty of gay people who don't have the highest household incomes. Yes, the gay market is lucrative but while the data will show that in general compared to the mainstream straight traveler they statistically earn more but that is not always the case.

How important is it to get your terminology straight? So much so that the National Lesbian and Gay Journalists Association (NLGJA) created the world's foremost glossary with words specific to the GLBT community. The NLGJA *Stylebook Supplement on Lesbian, Gay, Bisexual and Transgender Terminology* is published here with permission from the NLGJA.

The NLGJA *Stylebook Supplement on Lesbian, Gay, Bisexual and Transgender Terminology* reflects the NLGJA's mission of inclusive media coverage of lesbian, gay, bisexual and transgender people that leads people to a better understanding of the GLBT community. The stylebook is not a dictionary of gay terms, it does include definitions on words and phrases that have become common.

I am a proud member of NLGJA and this organization played an instrumental role in the development of Philadelphia's gay tourism campaign. NLGJA provides unparalleled professional resources for journalists and this is also particularly useful for tourism professionals, especially for those working in communications and media relations. This organization has its headquarters in Washington, D.C., and there are 1300 NLGJA members and 25 local chapters around the United States.[10] NLGJA provides educational and networking opportunities ideal for tourism professionals. NLGJA offers associate memberships that are very affordable and there is annual convention held each year. Past host cities have been Philadelphia, Miami and Brooklyn. For those destinations looking to promote their city as gay-friendly, one important step is to host the NLGJA convention. Gail Shister from *The Philadelphia Inquirer*, is a noted journalist; she invited me to join NLGJA, and therefore, I invite you to join.

Without the efforts of NLGJA, the extraordinary rise in gay tourism between 2003 and today could not be possible because this community would remain so misunderstood and so stigmatized in the media and in the minds of people that few destinations would ever actively woo this market without fear of backlash and negative publicity. NLGJA is perhaps the most effective organization in shaping the image of GLBT people. Seemingly, everyday there is a news story about gay marriage, gay rights, gays in the military or any number of political, social, legal or religious debates on the status of gay people in the United States and the world. We are living in a world dominated by media. No longer is the GLBT community invisible and in the closet. They are out and they are in the media.

The members of the NLGJA continue to work diligently inside and outside of the newsroom to provide people with accurate information on the GLBT community. This organization works to get appropriate terminology used in media reports and also looks to dispel bias in news coverage.

NLGJA and its members have been instrumental in how to accurately describe and cover the HIV crisis as a global health issue. They have also educated newsrooms about differences between being gay and pedophilia during the Catholic Church priest scandals. They worked on the coverage of Matthew Sheppard, coming out stories of celebrities and even early coverage of gay tourism. In short, this organization is the primary image-maker of the gay community.

I think this example of an open letter that NLGJA sent to newsrooms around the United States provides additional insight into how to use terminology that you will not find in the glossary of terms.[11]

Dear Fellow Journalist:

Today, Tuesday, November 29th (2005), the Vatican issued new guidance to its dioceses on the role of gay men in the Catholic Church. Members of the National Lesbian & Gay Journalists Association (NLGJA) have noticed a number of inaccurate and unfair portrayals of gay men in the reporting of this document, which has been widely leaked in advance of today's release date. Some of those reports have included references to sexual "preferences," and reporting without verification parishioner statements that most of the priests involved in the Church's sex-abuse scandal were gay. Also, factually incorrect opinions that assert a cause-and-effect link between gay men and pedophilia are being reported without challenge.

As journalists and leaders of NLGJA, we acknowledge our job to report assertions by Catholic officials that the presence of gay clergy has resulted in sexual abuse cases, and even stated beliefs that link pedophilia and gay men. However, if similar statements were made about other minority and stigmatized groups, reporters and editors would feel obliged to find sources to challenge those allegations, and to otherwise provide factual information to do so. NLGJA urges that the same professional standards be applied to stories concerning lesbian, gay, bisexual and transgender people.

In addition, it's important to point out that the term "sexual preference" implies that sexuality – whether heterosexual, homosexual or bisexual – is the result of a conscious choice. That is a politically charged suggestion. In order to be accurate and neutral, journalists should use terms such as "sexual orientation," "sexuality" or "sexual identity" as appropriate.

When news organizations cover instances of sexual abuse by heterosexual adults against children of the opposite sex, they are not cast as stories about sexual orientation. They are accurately reported as crimes against children. News coverage about the sex abuse scandal in the Catholic Church has done more to link gay men with pedophilia than any other story in decades. Without balance, expert inquiry and opposing views, such charges can create long-lasting and inaccurate ideas that can damage the lives of LGBT people. As journalists we owe it to our readers and viewers to uphold a basic practice of our profession: Get all sides of the story and provide our audiences with all the facts.

NLGJA has a number of online resources to assist journalists in covering LGBT people and issues, including our *Stylebook Supplement on Lesbian, Gay, Bisexual & Transgender Terminology* and our *Journalists Toolbox*.

Sincerely,

Eric Hegedus
NLGJA National President

NLGJA has written a stylebook to help guide journalists, public relations professionals and marketers use terminology correctly. With their permission, I have included a few key definitions. The stylebook was created by the members of NLJGA.

Finally, in addition to NLGJA, there are many professionals, conferences and online resources to help you learn more about gay and lesbian terminology. Here are few of the top resources for you to consider:

Human Rights Campaign (HRC), founded in 1980, works to educate the public on a wide array of topics affecting GLBT Americans, including relationship recognition, workplace, family and health issues.[12] The HRC Foundation engages in research and provides public education and programming. HRC's *Corporate Equality Index* rates companies on a scale from zero to 100 based on their treatment of GLBT workers, customers and investors. In 2006, 138 companies received the top score.

The IGLTA is the world's leading travel trade association committed to growing and enhancing its members' gay and lesbian tourism business through education, promotion and networking.[13] Founded in 1983, with 25 founding members, the IGLTA is today a 1000-plus member strong and growing organization of gay-, lesbian- and community-friendly travel professionals. Each year, IGLTA holds an annual conference.

The Gay and Lesbian Alliance Against Defamation (GLAAD) is dedicated to promoting and ensuring fair, accurate and inclusive representation of people and events in the media as a means of eliminating homophobia and discrimination based on gender identity and sexual orientation.[14]

The National Gay and Lesbian Chamber of Commerce, created in November 2002 by cofounders Chance Mitchell and Justin Nelson, is a broad-based coalition, representative of the various interests of GLBT-owned and GLBT-friendly businesses, professionals, and students of business for the purpose of promoting economic growth and prosperity of its members.[15]

The International Conference on Gay and Lesbian Tourism, produced by Community Marketing, Inc., is held annually in a new host city. The conference is perfect for those just exploring gay tourism marketing and for the seasoned professional looking to exchange new ideas.[16]

Now, have fun and test your knowledge! Practice using these words in a sentence. For an up-to-date list, be sure to visit the NLGJA website at nlgja.com. (Reprinted with permission from the NLGJA, nlgja.org.)

AIDS: Acquired Immune Deficiency Syndrome, a medical condition that compromises the human immune system, leaving the body defenseless against opportunistic infections. Some medical treatments can slow the rate at which the immune system is weakened. Do not use the term "full-blown AIDS." Individuals may be HIV-positive but not have AIDS. Avoid "AIDS sufferer" and "AIDS victim." Use "people with AIDS" or, if the context is medical, "AIDS patients." See *HIV*.

Bisexual: As a noun, an individual who may be attracted to both sexes. As an adjective, of or relating to sexual and affectional attraction to both sexes. Does not presume non-monogamy.

Civil union: The state of Vermont began this formal recognition of lesbian and gay relationships in July 2000. A civil union provides same-sex couples some rights available to married couples in areas such as state taxes, medical decisions and estate planning.

Closeted, in the closet: Refers to a person who wishes to keep secret his or her sexual orientation or gender identity.

Coming out: Short for "coming out of the closet." Accepting and letting others know of one's previously hidden sexual orientation or gender identity. See *closeted and outing*.

Commitment ceremony: A formal, marriage-like gathering that recognizes the declaration of members of the same sex to each other. Same-sex marriages are not legally recognized by the U.S. government. See *marriage*.

Cross-dresser: Preferred term for person who wears clothing most often associated with members of the opposite sex. Not necessarily connected to sexual orientation.

Cruising: Visiting places where opportunities exist to meet potential sex partners. Not exclusively a gay phenomenon.

Domestic partner: Unmarried partners who live together. Domestic partners may be of opposite sexes or the same sex. They may register in some counties, municipalities and states and receive some of the same benefits accorded married couples. The term is typically used in connection with legal and insurance matters. See gay/lesbian relationships.

Don't ask, don't tell: Shorthand for "Don't Ask, Don't Tell, Don't Pursue, Don't Harass," the military policy on gay men, lesbians and bisexuals. Under the policy, instituted in 1993, the military is not to ask service members about their sexual orientation, service members are not to tell others about their orientation, and the military is not to pursue rumors about members' sexual orientation. The shorthand is acceptable in headlines, but in text the full phrase adds important balance.

Down low: Usually refers to black men who secretly have sex with men, often while in relationships with women, but do not identify as gay or bisexual. Sometimes abbreviated as DL. Use with caution, as people generally do not identify themselves using this term.

Drag: Attire of the opposite sex.

Drag performers: Entertainers who dress and act in styles typically associated with the opposite sex (drag queen for men, drag king for women). Not synonymous with transgender or cross-dressing.

Dyke: Originally a pejorative term for a lesbian, it is now being reclaimed by some lesbians. Caution: still extremely offensive when used as an epithet.

"ex-gay" (adj.): Describes the movement, mostly rooted in conservative religions, that aims to change the sexual attraction of individuals from same-sex to opposite-sex.

Fag, faggot: Originally a pejorative term for a gay male, it is now being reclaimed by some gay men. Caution: still extremely offensive when used as an epithet.

FTM: Acronym for "female to male." A transgender person who, at birth or by determination of parents or doctors, has a biological identity of female but a gender identity of male. Those who have undergone surgery are sometimes described as "post-op FTMs" (for post-operative). See *gender identity and intersex*.

Gay: An adjective that has largely replaced "homosexual" in referring to men who are sexually and affectionally attracted to other men. Avoid using as a singular noun. For women, "lesbian" is preferred. To include both, use "gay men and lesbians." In headlines where space is an issue, "gays" is acceptable to describe both.

Gay/lesbian relationships: Gay, lesbian and bisexual people use various terms to describe their commitments. Ask the individual what term he or she prefers, if possible. If not, "partner" is generally acceptable.

Gender identity: An individual's emotional and psychological sense of being male or female. Not necessarily the same as an individual's biological identity.

Heterosexism: Presumption that heterosexuality is universal and/or superior to homosexuality. Also: prejudice, bias or discrimination based on such presumptions.

HIV: Human immunodeficiency virus. The virus that causes AIDS. "HIV virus" is redundant. "HIV-positive" means being infected with HIV but not necessarily having AIDS. AIDS doctors and researchers are using the term "HIV disease" more because there are other types of acquired immune deficiencies caused by toxins and rare but deadly diseases that are unrelated to what we now call AIDS. See AIDS.

Homo: Pejorative term for homosexual. Avoid.

Homophobia: Fear, hatred or dislike of homosexuality, gay men and lesbians.

Homosexual: As a noun, a person who is attracted to members of the same sex. As an adjective, of or relating to sexual and affectional attraction to a member of the same sex. Use only if "heterosexual" would be used in parallel constructions, such as in medical contexts. For other usages, see gay and lesbian.

Intersex (adj.): People born with sex chromosomes, external genitalia or an internal reproductive system that is not considered standard for either male or female. Parents and physicians usually will determine the sex of the child, resulting in surgery or hormone treatment. Many intersex adults seek an end to this practice.

Lesbian: Preferred term, both as a noun and as an adjective, for women who are sexually and affectionally attracted to other women. Some women prefer to be called "gay" rather than "lesbian"; when possible, ask the subject what term she prefers.

LGBT: Acronym for "lesbian, gay, bisexual and transgender."

Lifestyle: An inaccurate term sometimes used to describe the lives of gay, lesbian, bisexual and transgender people. Sexual orientation may be part of a broader lifestyle but is not one in itself, just as there is no "straight" lifestyle. Avoid.

Lover: A gay, lesbian, bisexual or heterosexual person's sexual partner. "Partner" is generally acceptable. See gay/lesbian relationships.

MSM: Acronym for "men who have sex with men." Term used usually in communities of color to describe men who secretly have sex with other men while maintaining relationships with women. Not synonymous with "bisexual." See down low.

Marriage: Advocates for the right to marry seek the legal rights and obligations of marriage, not a variation of it. Often, the most neutral approach is to avoid any adjective modifying the word "marriage." For the times in which a distinction is necessary, "marriage for same-sex couples" is preferable in stories. When there is a need for shorthand description (such as in headline writing), "same-sex marriage" is preferred because it is more inclusive and more accurate than "gay."

MTF: Acronym for "male to female." A transgender person who, at birth or by determination of parents or doctors, has a biological identity of male but a gender identity of female. Those who have undergone surgery are sometimes described as "post-op MTFs" (for post-operative). See gender identity and intersex.

Openly gay/lesbian: As a modifier, "openly" is usually not relevant; its use should be restricted to instances in which the public awareness of an individual's sexual orientation is germane. Examples: Harvey Milk was the first openly gay San Francisco supervisor. "Ellen" was the first sitcom to feature an openly lesbian lead character. "Openly" is preferred over "avowed," "admitted," "confessed" or "practicing."

Outing (from "out of the closet"): Publicly revealing the sexual orientation or gender identity of an individual who has chosen to keep that information private. Also a verb: The magazine outed the senator in a front-page story. See coming out and closeted.

Pink triangle: Now a gay pride symbol, it was the symbol gay men were required to wear in Nazi concentration camps during World War II. Lesbians sometimes also use a black triangle.

Practicing: Avoid this term to describe someone's sexual orientation or gender identity. Use "sexually active" as a modifier in circumstances when public awareness of an individual's behavior is germane.

Pride (Day and/or march): Short for gay/lesbian pride, this term is commonly used to indicate the celebrations commemorating the Stonewall Inn riots of June 28, 1969. Pride events typically take place in June. See Stonewall.

Queen: Originally a pejorative term for an effeminate gay man. Still considered offensive when used as an epithet.

Queer: Originally a pejorative term for gay, now being reclaimed by some gay, lesbian, bisexual and transgender people as a self-affirming umbrella term. Still extremely offensive when used as an epithet.

Rainbow flag: A flag of six equal horizontal stripes (red, orange, yellow, green, blue and violet) signifying the diversity of the lesbian, gay, bisexual and transgender communities.

Safe sex, safer sex: Sexual practices that minimize the possible transmission of HIV and other infectious agents.

Sexual orientation: Innate sexual attraction. Use this term instead of "sexual preference." See *lifestyle*.

Sexual preference: Avoid. See *sexual orientation*.

Sodomy: Collective term for various sexual acts that some states have deemed illegal. Not synonymous with homosexuality or sex between gay men. The legal definition of sodomy is different from state to state; in some states, sodomy laws have applied to sexual acts practiced by heterosexuals. The U.S. Supreme Court decided in June 2003 that state sodomy laws targeting private, consensual sex between adult same-sex or opposite-sex partners violate the U.S. Constitution's due process clause.

Special rights: Politically charged term used by opponents of civil rights for gay people. Avoid. "Gay civil rights," "equal rights" or "gay rights" are alternatives.

Stonewall: The Stonewall Inn tavern in New York City's Greenwich Village was the site of several nights of raucous protests after a police raid on June 28, 1969. Although not the nation's first gay civil rights demonstration, Stonewall is now regarded as the birth of the modern gay civil rights movement.

Straight (adj.): Heterosexual; describes a person whose sexual and affectional attraction is to someone of the opposite sex.

Transgender (adj): An umbrella term that refers to people whose biological and gender identity or expression may not be the same. This can include preoperative, postoperative or nonoperative transsexuals, female and male cross-dressers, drag queens or kings, female or male impersonators, and intersex individuals. If an individual prefers to be called transsexual, drag queen or king, intersex, etc., use that term. When writing about a transgender person, use the name and personal pronouns that are consistent with the way the individual lives publicly.

Transition: The process by which one alters one's sex. This may include surgery, hormone therapy and changes of legal identity.

Transsexual (n.): An individual who identifies himself or herself as a member of the opposite sex and who acquires the physical characteristics of the opposite sex. Individual can be of any sexual orientation. To determine accurate use of names or personal pronouns, use the name and sex of the individual at the time of the action.

Transvestite: Avoid. See *cross-dresser*.

Two spirit: An American Indian believed to possess a mixture of masculine and feminine spirits. Some identify as gay, lesbian, bisexual or transgender. Should not be used as a blanket term for LGBT American Indians.

Case study

The Key West Business Guild

Stephen Murray-Smith, President International Gay and Lesbian Travel Association, Florida Keys & Key West

> Sleepy allure and isolated location be damned – Key West has been reinventing itself. With super-charming architecture, beautiful guesthouses (some 100 percent gay, including Pearl's, "the Ritz of guesthouses for women"), a vibrant art scene and a nightlife that belies its size (think late hours, adult entertainment and dancers), this end-of-the-rainbow locale is fast becoming an almost boutique gay destination.
>
> Planetout.com 2006

For decades, visiting Key West on a "coming out" trip has been almost a rite of passage for gays and lesbians.

During the 1970s, Key West was experiencing difficult economic times, but at the same time, the island was gaining popularity with gays and lesbians, which contributed to the renovation and restoration of the historic Old Town district. Tennessee Williams was one of the earliest notable gay residents of Key West, and his love of the island brought many friends and colleagues to visit, and to eventually reside on the island.

Since the late 1950s, Duval Street was known for its number and variety of bars, some featuring strippers who were lesbians, and others featuring entertainers who were drag queens.

From 1948 to 1954, the Tradewinds was one of the original gay bars. Its back door opened up to the ever-popular Simonton

Court guesthouses. The Mermaid lounge, another gay bar, was located in the historic La Concha Hotel. The ever-popular Key West Monster appeared on Front Street and was duplicated in New York's Greenwich Village several years later.

In the mid 1970s, Tony Falcone and Bill Konkel opened Fast Buck Freddie's tropical department store. Following in their footsteps, a towel boutique – Towels of Key West – opened, joining other gay-owned restaurants and bars, which contributed to the resurgence of business on Duval Street. Gingerbread Square Gallery, established in 1974 by Lee Dodez and Richard Heyman, was the art venue that launched Key West's development into a major center of visual art.

In 1984, Heyman was elected mayor of the City of Key West, becoming the first openly gay man elected to lead a city in the United States. He won the election because he was the best candidate, not because he was gay. Heyman's tenure as mayor saw the continued growth and popularity of Key West with the GLBT communities.

The island coined the term "gay guesthouse," and one of the first guesthouses, The Banyan, was frequented by such celebrities as Leonard Bernstein, Jerry Herman and Calvin Klein. Other guesthouses followed, including Big Ruby's and the late famous porn star Casey Donovan's guesthouse, Casa Donovan, Alexander's Guesthouse, the Lime House, the Lighthouse Court, the Island House, Oasis, the Garden House, author's guesthouse and the Rainbow House, to name a few.

Telling the world about Key West

Key West began to recognize the popularity of its many gay and lesbian guesthouses, restaurants and bars. At the same time, gay business owners recognized that greater diversity awareness was needed and that the time had come for the gay community to become a voice in local politics. After all, the overall tourism industry benefited from the gay market.

In 1977, the Key West Business Guild formed to answer that need.

Composed of guesthouse owners and retailers, the guild was formed to tell the world about an island, located at the southern end of continental America, where gays could be themselves.

The guild, along with one of its founders – advertising agency Impressions Unlimited – became the catalyst for cooperative advertising in the first gay publications in the country.

The Advocate's early years as a newspaper (some remember the pink pull-out section) saw half- and full-page advertisements featuring guesthouses and businesses in Key West. At the heart of the advertising program was the realization that gay men and women needed and wanted a place to go to be accepted – something that's still a challenge in many communities. The ads told the story of a place where you could let your hair down and be yourself, a place where gay was okay.

Since its inception, the guild operated a mail-fulfillment program that responded to callers who read ads in various publications. The program operated years before the Internet became a more efficient way to communicate with potential visitors. During peak calling periods, more than 1500 information packages were mailed each week. The guild still maintains direct-mail fulfillment, which is in addition to more than 6000 brochure downloads monthly from its websites.

In 1995, the guild opened a gay and lesbian visitors' center in the heart of Old Town Key West. Operating five days a week, the center provided a contact point for visitors and an information and referral service. Brochures from guild members were distributed to visitors. A map and directory of guild members was distributed to all member businesses to be provided to visitors. The gay visitor center now is open seven days a week from 9 a.m. to 5 p.m. and receives hundreds of visitors weekly.

In the early 1990s, the guild, through members' efforts, became part of the Florida Keys Tourist Development Council's (TDC's) mainstream marketing program. Initially, the funding was just a few thousand dollars.

During subsequent years, the budget has increased to a six-figure amount. In addition to advertising, TDC funds are allocated through the Keys public relations office for GLBT-specific media research trips, trade shows and a part-time PR professional assigned exclusively to the market. For more than 10 years, the TDC has retained a part-time GLBT sales manager. The position promotes the destination domestically and internationally to the market.

Eight years ago, the Florida Keys booth at London's World Travel Market raised the first ever rainbow flag to be displayed. Three months later, the Keys flew the rainbow flag at Europe's premier travel market, ITB. Today at ITB, there are many booths promoting to the gay market.

In 2003, during Pridefest Key West, the world's longest rainbow flag was unfurled down Key West's Duval Street. The celebration was the 25th anniversary of both the creation of the rainbow flag and the inception of the Key West Business Guild. More than 2500 people – gay and straight – joined in to carry the flag from the Gulf of Mexico to the Atlantic Ocean. Stretching more than 8000 feet and weighing three tons, the giant flag was sewn with its original eight colors by its creator, Gilbert Baker.

As a symbol of diversity, the big flag was cut up and parts of it are still carried in pride parades throughout the world.

A documentary, "Key West City of Colors," was produced to capture the acceptance and diversity of the community, as well as to document the stitching and presentation of the world's longest rainbow flag.

Sharing the good work

In 1983, the Key West Business Guild joined with gay travel professionals around the United States to form the International Gay Travel Association. Impressions Unlimited, the Key West advertising agency, became headquarters for the IGTA, maintaining membership records and producing newsletters. As the organization grew, the "L" was added, changing the name to International Gay and Lesbian Travel Association.

Through efforts of its founders, the organization achieved not-for-profit status and continued membership development. Key West hosted the organization's largest familiarization trip, with 125 attendees. Ten years ago, the board chose to employ an executive director and relocate the headquarters to Fort Lauderdale, Florida. However, Key West maintains a strong presence with the group, having guild members serve on the board of directors and as president.

Where Key West is today

In the spring of 2005, the Key West Business Guild began to plan a survey of gay and lesbian visitors, and potential visitors, to Key West. The guild identified four primary objectives:

1) To measure levels of visitor satisfaction with the process of seeking and obtaining information on Key West.

2) To understand the motivation of visitors who come to Key West and factors contributing to visitors' decision not to come to the Key West.

3) To evaluate the experience of gay and lesbian visitors to Key West.

4) To validate the guild's understanding of gay and lesbian demographics.

The target respondents were vacationers with a propensity toward visiting Key West – that is, potential and actual Key West visitors who had sought information on Key West gay and lesbian travel.

The survey was sent to 3000 potential and actual visitors via e-mail. Respondents were then directed to a website hosted by Survey Monkey to complete the 27-question survey. The guild received 727 responses.

The results were positive. An overwhelming majority of respondents, both recent visitors (within one year) and nonvisitors, or those who had visited more than a year ago, gave Key West a positive rating as a destination (96 percent recent visitors, 95 percent nonvisitor/visited more than a year ago). The response most chosen in each group was the highest possible rating of "great." Visitors were most satisfied with the atmosphere of the island, which they described as accepting, laid-back and friendly. Nonvisitors/visitors of more than a year ago shared the perception of recent visitors that Key West's most positive attribute is its atmosphere.

Respondents were given a series of other destinations popular with GLBT travelers, both national and international, and were asked to select those to which they had also traveled within the past year. Thirty-nine percent of respondents reported visiting at least one other gay-friendly destination besides Key West in the past year. The destination chosen by the most respondents was Fort Lauderdale (48.5 percent).

The destinations written under "Other" were both international, including Amsterdam, Paris and Berlin, and domestic, including West Palm Beach, Orlando and Portland. Here are the results:

Visitation to other destinations

Area	Count	Percent of responses	Percent of cases
New York	35	9.0	26.9
San Francisco	22	5.6	16.9
London	11	2.8	8.5
Other big city destination	54	13.8	41.5
Provincetown	15	3.8	11.5
Palm Springs	12	3.1	9.2
Rehoboth Beach	10	2.6	7.7
Other resort destination	22	5.6	16.9
Fort Lauderdale	**63**	**16.1**	**48.5**
South Beach	35	9.0	26.9
Other Florida destination	56	14.3	43.1
Other adventure destination	14	3.6	10.8
Other	33	8.4	25.4

Once the guild had reviewed the responses from the original survey, the question arose of whether the overwhelming positive perception of Key West was skewed, as the respondents had already demonstrated a propensity toward visiting the island. That is, the survey group that had been selected had previously sought information on visiting Key West.

Seeking to corroborate its survey findings by broadening its response pool, the guild used the popular blog website www.andrewsullivan.com, by providing a link on the site to their survey. That generated 133 survey responses, with approximately half of those responding being gay. Next, in an effort to increase female response rates, the guild utilized an opt-in e-mail database of the lesbian website www.lesbiannation.com, and received 751 responses.

As one might expect, there were much lower rates of recent visitation among the Andrew Sullivan group and the Lesbian Nation group than the Guild/TDC group that had shown a propensity toward a Key West vacation.

What was unexpected, and served to further validate the results of the original survey, was that the overwhelming majority of respondents from the Andrew Sullivan group and the Lesbian Nation group had a positive perception of Key West. This was true whether the respondent had recently visited the destination, had not visited or not recently visited.

The attribute of Key West that was cited as most positive among recent visitors for both groups was also the atmosphere, again described as laid-back, gay-friendly and accepting.

These results suggest that the respondents' perceptions of Key West have been influenced through advertising, personal experience or word of mouth and that their perception is in alignment with the message that Key West is a place where visitors can "come as they are" and have a positive vacation experience.

This is exactly the message that Key West has shared with gay and lesbian travelers for over 30 years. Many cities and businesses work to achieve the mix that this tiny island has offered its visitors. Much of what Key West offers is a lifestyle, which seems to come naturally.

Notes

1. International Gay and Lesbian Travel Association, IGLTA.com, July, 31, 2006.
2. Baker, Gilbert, "Let Them Talk", television interview, Manhattan Neighborhood Network, Channel 56, hosts DeRiezo, Moossy, May 11, 2006, intervideo.google.com/videoplay?docid=3959060154459763874.

3. Baker, Gilbert, "Let Them Talk", television interview, Manhattan Neighborhood Network, Channel 56, hosts DeRiezo, Moossy, May 11, 2006, intervideo.google.com/videoplay?docid= 3959060154459763874.
4. Gay and Lesbian Tourism Profile 2006, Community Marketing Inc., San Francisco, CA.
5. The U.S. Gay and Lesbian Market, Witeck–Combs Communications and Packaged Facts, February 14, 2006.
6. Kaminsky, Gregg, R Family Vacations, in-person interview, Philadelphia, PA, September 8, 2006.
7. Holden, LoAnn, writer, in-person interview, Miami, Florida, September 9, 2006.
8. Salvato, Ed, Planet Out Inc., in-person interview, South Beach, Miami, September 9, 2006.
9. Levitz, Meryl, Greater Philadelphia Tourism Marketing, in-person interview, Philadelphia, PA, September 5, 2006.
10. National Association of Lesbian and Gay Journalists Association, nlgja.com, March 13, 2006.
11. National Association of Lesbian and Gay Journalists Association, nlgja.com, March 13, 2006.
12. Human Rights Campaign, HRC.org, October 2006.
13. International Gay and Lesbian Travel Association, IGLTA.com, July 31, 2006.
14. Gay and Lesbian Alliance Against Defamation, glaad.org, October 2006.
15. National Gay and Lesbian Chamber of Commerce, nglcc.org, October 2006.
16. Community Marketing Inc., communitymarketinginc.com, October 2006.

The economic power of gay tourism: it is about good business not a political or social statement

At the jammed packed press conference, the Greater Philadelphia Tourism Marketing Corporation (GPTMC) and the Philadelphia Gay Tourism Caucus launched Philly's gay tourism campaign, Philadelphia Get Your History Straight and Your Nightlife Gay®. The event was held at the William

Way Gay, Lesbian, Bisexual and Transgender Community Center in November 2003. A private nonprofit organization, GPTMC's mission is about bringing business to Philadelphia through tourism not social change. Meryl Levitz, president and CEO, knew to succeed we needed to be armed with research to back up the claim that gay tourism was a strategic business decision that would bring huge economic rewards to Philadelphia. As it would turn out, Philly was the first city in the United States to commission a research study specific to a destination.

With the audience of gay and straight supporters seated in rows of rainbow-colored chairs (how gay-friendly is that!), Tom Roth from Community Marketing, Inc. (CMI), presented the results of research that GPTMC commissioned. The results that proved that gay tourism was a matter of good business and that cities that did not extend an invitation to gay travelers were losing their share of a $54 billion travel market. Tom let the statistics speak for GPTMC. Gay travelers take more trips than straight travelers, they spend more and they earn more.[1]

The research was an important tool because no one wanted gay tourism to be confused with political, social or religious controversy. Every news media outlet covered the press conference including the Associated Press, but would the news media agree with our premise and confine the discussion of Philly's gay tourism campaign to good business?

The 6 p.m. television news coverage was universally clear that Philly was going after the gay travel dollar. Whew! Now, the stage was set. The tone of Philadelphia's campaign would remain about good business. For years to come, destinations around the world would use research to help launch their tourism campaigns.

However, while research, may help make the case for gay tourism programs, the challenge facing all tourism professionals is that gay travelers remain among the most underresearched group. Most mainstream travel research resources including Global Insight (economic impact), Shifflet, TNS and Longwoods don't have in-depth information on gay travelers.[2] It wasn't until December 2006 that the Travel Industry of America (TIA) released its findings on that organization's first study on gay and lesbian tourism.

This vacuum of information on gay travelers gave private companies like Community Marketing, Inc., in San Francisco and Witeck–Combs Communications in Washington D.C. the opportunity to become pioneers in gay tourism research and gay consumer research. It is essential that there be credible research for the gay travel market to continue to mature and to be taken seriously.

How do you ask the "gay" question?

Why does gay tourism remain so underresearched? According to Deborah Diamond, Ph.D., director of research for GPTMC, "gay tourism remains in a research ghetto".[3]

> People haven't figured out how to ask the question are you are gay? Asking are you gay is still very private and a sensitive subject. How do you know how to ask the question the right way? You can't just go up to people and ask them if they are gay. If you alienate people with the questions that you ask they either won't answer your survey or they won't be honest with you. That is why they put the household income question at the end.

"How do you deal with things private or sensitive is a huge issue," she said. "One day the gay question won't be considered private or sensitive but right now it is."

Dr. Diamond goes on to say that the bulk of the research that is out there is based on people who are self-identified as GLBT and come forward through existing gay media channels or venues predominantly visited by openly gay people. It is far better to connect with GLBT travelers in all paths, not just gay media, to know what they are thinking. While this data is extraordinarily useful and the best that is out there right now, she cautions that it is ideal to have a random sample of GLBT travelers to get true knowledge.

All research ordinarily has merit and gives us more knowledge. It must be noted that some of the research in this chapter comes from databases with self-identified gay travelers. Some of this information is based on nonrandom, convenience samples. Largely, the data in this chapter was created by using lists of people who in some way volunteered to be surveyed because they happened to be interested in gay travel or very strongly identified as GLBT. This information, while not random, is still very valuable because the question asked was are you gay? And in reality, some would argue that information from self-identified gay people is the most valuable to marketers because the travel decisions of people who identify as GLBT can be more readily influenced. It is very difficult to market to those travelers who are "in the closet" or don't consider themselves to be part of the GLBT community or who usually do not read gay magazines, visit gay websites or attend gay community events and gatherings.

Dr. Diamond acknowledges four limitations to most GLBT research studies:

1. Gay travelers have been shut out or perhaps invisible from traditional research because asking if you are gay is such a sensitive question. Also, GLBT remained controversial for such a long time that researchers were hesitant to even engage in a gay travel study.

2. Gay research is still in many ways in its early stages. Research in the travel industry is still developing baselines for the gay and lesbian traveler. It takes a couple of rounds of research to identify patterns that can be defined and then influenced by marketing.

3. Gay travelers themselves are still identifying who they are when it comes to travel. For example, are gay people always gay travelers every time they take a trip no matter what the purpose? Do gay people travel differently when they are on their company business compared to when they are paying for the trip themselves? Or, do they make travel decisions as do business travelers who just happen to be gay? How does being out at work or with family impact those travel decisions? Slowly as the gay travel market matures, more gay travelers will answer those questions, researchers will measure those responses and it will impact how marketers influence those decisions.

4. There is plenty of consumer research, but there still remains a lack of consumer insight. The research studies are filled with lots of facts and figures. Yet, we still do not know the person that we are talking about. Who is this person? When are they comfortable as gay travelers and when are they not? Is there a difference between a 60-year-old gay man and a 20-year-old gay man in their travel patterns? Do they feel different or do they not? Smart qualitative studies and perhaps lots of focus groups will address these questions. There is a need for broader and in-depth consumer insights.

All of this is not to say that there is no great information out there. On the contrary, there is a vast amount of information that it is essential to your gay tourism campaigns. To ignore what is out there would be irresponsible.

However, because gay research is still in its infancy, little data exists that specifically addresses the niches within the niche such as gay families, gay sports, transgender or bisexual travelers. Additionally, there are gay travelers who totally identify as gay but don't travel as a gay person so it is even harder to research them. They are the invisible gay traveler.

Gay consumer research overview

If you want to know how the GLBT community spends their money, ask Bob Witeck and Wesley Combs (and I'm happy to add that Wesley is a fellow native Philadelphian). Since 1993, Witeck–Combs Communications has provided expert marketing communications counsel to Fortune 500 companies in their strategies to reach the gay consumer market. One of their longstanding clients is American Airlines.

In September 2006, Bob and Wes released their first book called *Business Inside Out: Capturing Millions of Brand Loyal Consumers* (Kaplan Publishing). In this book, Bob and Wesley present in-depth consumer marketing research and present case studies from Fortune 500 companies that market their product to the GLBT consumer.

Research studies estimate between 6 percent and 7 percent of the U.S. adult population self-identify as gay, lesbian or bisexual, equating to roughly 15 million adult gay men and lesbians over the age of 18.[4] By gender, the breakdown would be approximately 8 million men and 6 million women. Same-sex couples also were found to live in 99.3 percent of all U.S. counties.[5]

Witeck–Combs, along with Packaged Facts, has also published the fourth edition of the "The U.S. Gay and Lesbian Market," a comprehensive research report that aggregates available public data to provide in-depth demographic profiles, consumer behaviors and the annual barometer of purchasing power of the adult gay men and lesbians living in the United States.

The total buying power of the U.S. GLBT population in 2006 was estimated to be $641 billion, up from $610 billion in 2005. By 2008, total buying power of the GLBT population will exceed $800 billion. Buyer power represents the amount of money after taxes and obligations that can be spent on things like home mortgages or rent, car and transportation expenses, utility bills, food, entertainment and travel.[6]

Bob notes that "buying power is customarily what we have left to spend after paying our taxes." He adds quickly that it is challenging to directly compare with other minority populations, given that there is obvious overlap and populations are not mutually exclusive. It stands to reason that gay men and lesbians also are black, white and brown, and they come from all ethnic backgrounds. Gay households compare well with other minority groups but would not be deemed uniquely affluent. Same-sex couples, on average and more than heterosexual couples, tend to have both partners working, have fewer children and happen to be more male and more urban – both indicators of slightly higher earnings.

The gay market compares well with other minority groups. Asian Americans have an annual buying power of $344 billion; African Americans $688 billion and Hispanic Americans $653 billion annual buying power.[7] It is awkward to compare the gay market to other minority groups because there is overlap and they are mutually exclusive. Remember, there are gay Asians, gay African Americans and gay Hispanics.

"Gay buying behaviors are more important than the total buying figure," explains Bob.[8] "The buying power serves a useful purpose, to get people's attention and that can be a good thing. It reminds people that gay and lesbian people make measurable contributions to the economy. The GLBT community controls a lot of money."

Bob offers this example. When is a gay Hispanic man making buying choices as a gay consumer and when is he a Hispanic consumer? The answer is likely both. At different times, he may be influenced more by one part of his identity, background and experience than the other part. When he goes to the supermarket, he probably is more influenced by Hispanic culture and familiar foods he grew up with at home. When shopping for clothes or for travel he may be somewhat more influenced by his gay identity and sense of fashion. In his travel decisions he may want to be surrounded with other gay people, so he might choose an all-gay cruise or take his partner to Key West to get away. Conversely, when he buys dish washing liquid, he is probably more influenced by what his mother purchased for her kitchen.

According to the Witeck–Combs data, gay and lesbian consumers are brand-loyal, trendsetters, fair-minded and online more than heterosexuals. The question marketers really need research to answer is should they be doing differently or keep doing the same if they want to communicate with gay men and lesbians? Does this segment respond to different marketing cues? Take for example, Bridgestone Tires. There is nothing gay about tires, but advertising in gay media does communicate gay-friendliness.

Gay travel research overview

A recognized authority in gay travel research is Community Marketing, Incorporate (CMI). Tom Roth and his team recognized the influence of gay travel before most. Tom very wisely began to measure and track gay travel more than a decade ago. He is perhaps the most quoted expert on gay travel research.

For 14 years, CMI has been collecting and analyzing data on gay travelers. It acknowledges that its research is based on self-identified gay travelers and has limitations. However, no other organization knows more about gay travel research. In October 2006, CMI released its 11th Annual Gay and Lesbian Tourism Profile 2006. CMI based its data and conclusions on 7500 self-identified gay and lesbian consumers who belong to gay mailing lists, subscribe to gay publications, visit gay websites or in some way elect to take a gay travel survey.

Safety, progressive politics (such as gay marriage) and even immigration (policies that don't discriminate against gay people) all play a factor in travel decisions. The latest research found that among gay travelers the top seven U.S. destinations are New York City, Las Vegas, San Francisco, Los Angeles-West Hollywood, Palm Springs, Fort Lauderdale and Chicago. The top seven European cities are London, Paris, Rome, Amsterdam, Barcelona, Florence and Venice ties with Berlin.[9]

As pointed out earlier in this chapter, methodology is important. Here is CMI's methodology for this latest study:

> During August 2006, Community Marketing, Inc. conducted an online survey of openly-identified lesbian, gay, bisexual and transgender adults. The goal for this study was to survey LGBT consumers regarding their travel habits and motivators, and to provide data and insight to the gay and lesbian tourism industry. With a sample size of 6,721, the margin of error is 1.2 percent at a 95 percent confidence interval. Respondents to this survey are subscribers to various Internet and print media, and therefore represent lesbians and gay men who can be reached using the media. Community Marketing has developed its survey pool over the last eleven years by partnering with leading media companies including Gay.com, PlanetOut.com, GayWired.com, LesbiaNation.com, Gay Travel News, Passport, Curve, Instinct, HX, Genre, and others. Subscribers to various email lists received an invitation to take a gay/lesbian travel survey; however, no attempt was made to pre-qualify the invitations to survey only people who travel. The incentive offered to respondents to complete the survey was one chance out of all respondents to win a $500 gift card. This methodology polls LGBT consumers who represent the target audience of gays and lesbians who can be reached using print and the Internet. We make no attempt in this survey to define the size of the LGBT population, nor to invade the privacy of our respondents by asking them to "out" themselves in a random survey, which as demonstrated in the 2000 U.S. Census, grossly underestimates the size of the gay population.

It should be kept in mind that the findings derive from those who identify openly as gay and subscribe lesbian and gay publications and websites. These results should not necessarily be extrapolated to the entire gay and lesbian population; however, these findings do provide guidance regarding the perceptions and opinions of "out" gay travelers who can be reached through gay websites and publications.

The following gay and lesbian travel demographics come directly from the CMI 2006 study:[10]

- Median household income of U.S. respondents is $79,000

- 35 percent of U.S. respondents live in households earning more than $100,000

- 71 percent of gay U.S. respondents hold a valid passport and 47 percent used it in the past year

- The median respondent spent $6300 on travel in the last year, about $1250 per trip

- 66 percent are college graduates and 31 percent hold a master's or doctorate degree

- 73 percent were gay men, 21 percent are lesbian and 5 percent are bisexual

- 54 percent are in relationships with a median duration lasting eight years, and 26 percent are in relationships that have some form of legal recognition (i.e., marriage, domestic partnership)

- 17 percent of lesbians and 4 percent of gay men between the ages of 30 and 60 have one or more children under 18 living with them.

The CMI 2006 gay travel statistics:[11]

- Gay and lesbian travelers took a median of five overnight trips in the last 12 months; 23 percent of the respondents took more than five leisure trips

- Respondents who traveled in the last year spent an average of 29 nights away from home, on average six nights per trip

- 92 percent of gays and lesbians purchased an airline ticket online last year

- Respondents spent a median of 15 nights in a hotel during the last year

- 44 percent said that having Internet service was important to their choice of hotel. It was the number one motivator
- 67 percent rented a car at least once in the last year
- 18 percent took a cruise within the last year

Hotels and the gay traveler[12]

CMI reports that 97 percent U.S. respondents spent at least one night away from home in the last 12 months. The CMI survey revealed that gay travelers spent on average 29 nights away from home, a median of six nights per trip.

- Leisure: 12 nights (median of 6 nights per trip)
- Personal: 9 nights (median of 4 nights per trip)
- Business: 8 nights (median of 8 nights per trip)

What factors influence a gay and a lesbian traveler when they choose a hotel? Forty-four percent told CMI that Internet access at their hotel was one of considerations in their hotel selection. Location is also important to gay and lesbian travelers, with 36 percent indicating that they prefer accommodations near the gay neighborhood. Food, fitness and relaxation are also important attributes to many lesbians and gay men when they stay in a hotel. A pool (35 percent), restaurant (28 percent), gym (25 percent) and room service (26 percent) are considered somewhat important. A "gay-knowledgeable" concierge was important to 22 percent, gay-marketed packages to 20 percent and "TAG Approved" to 20 percent.

Surprise, gay travelers like straight cruises[13]

Gay travel on straight cruises represents big business. Data within the 11th Annual Gay and Lesbian Travel Profile reveals a big surprise: gay and lesbian travelers prefer straight cruise vacations and they cruise more frequently than heterosexuals. Of the more than 4500 qualified responses, 65 percent of lesbians and gay men who took a cruise vacation in the last year have traveled on a mainstream (nongay) cruise. The survey also shows that 15 percent of gay travelers on straight cruises said they were part of an organized gay group; 21 percent of this survey's U.S. respondents took a mainstream cruise, 10 percent took a gay charter cruise and 4 percent traveled with a gay group aboard a mainstream cruise. More than three-quarters of those surveyed said that the itinerary influenced their decision to take a cruise (77 percent). Other factors in choosing a cruise vacation were as follows:

- Price (56 percent)

- Overall reputation of the cruise company (50 percent)

- Gay-friendly reputation of the cruise company (45 percent)

- Safety record (15 percent)

"There is huge sales opportunity for cruise lines and travel agents to sell cabins on straight cruises to gay travelers," said Tom Roth. "However, there is a challenge implied in the data. It's not just about advertising. In order to gain market share among the lucrative gay market, cruise lines must take active steps to ensure that their product is genuinely gay-friendly."

Gay men and lesbians fly regularly[14]

In the United States, gay men and lesbians flew 60 percent of the time, a median of six days in the last 12 months, and they flew much more than their straight counterparts. Air travel accounts for just 16 percent of travel in the United States for straight travelers, according to the TIA's Domestic Travel Market Report (2005).

Ninety-two percent of gay and lesbian U.S. respondents who flew indicated they had purchased airline tickets online in the last 12 months. Respondents who had flown at least once in the last year were most likely to have purchased tickets online through an online agency (such as Orbitz) or through a supplier website. Of the entire sample:

- 84 percent of respondents took at least one trip by air in the last 12 months

- 70 percent took 4 or more flights

- 56 percent took 6 or more

- 20 percent took 15 or more

- 11 percent took 30 or more

Online buying behavior[15]

At least 81 percent of U.S. respondents purchased travel components on the Internet in the last 12 months. Of all U.S. respondents 81 percent purchased airline tickets online, 80 percent purchased accommodations online, 65 percent rented a car using the Internet and 76 percent of those who took a cruise in the last 12 months indicated that they purchased at least one cruise online.

Gay travelers are booking more online than their straight counterparts. According to the TIA research report, "Travelers' Use of the Internet" (2005),[16] just 30 percent of the adult U.S. population used the Internet and made travel reservations/bookings online. Among the traveling adult U.S. population that number rose to 43 percent, but well short of the gay average.

Finally, advertising to the gay and lesbian market is profitable. Seventy-four percent of the respondents indicated that they are more likely to visit destinations where the government tourist office has a marketing campaign aimed at lesbians and gay men. Surprisingly, 37 percent said they will even "reward" destinations who advertise as gay-friendly by spending more money when they visit and 33 percent said they would stay longer.

To order a free copy of this report, call CMI at (415) 437–3800 or visit their website at www.communitymarketinginc.com.

The Travel Industry of America[17]

Perhaps surprisingly, it took until 2006 for the TIA to conduct that organization's first-ever representative national study on gay travelers. Conducted jointly with Harris Interactive and Witeck–Combs Communications, the study was based on a sample of more than 2000 self-identified U.S. GLBT adult travelers who completed a 25-minute online survey of travelers using Harris' GLBT Specialty Panel. The Harris Interactive GLBT Panel is unique because the sample is derived from many sources and is not specifically enlisted from targeted gay or lesbian websites, events or media. Helping TIA pioneer their research study were Visit Florida, Las Vegas, Hyatt Hotels, Expedia, Harrah's and Philadelphia. Perhaps, it was worth the wait. The findings of that study were announced in December 2006.

Here is the methodology that was reported by TIA and Witeck–Combs:

> The national online survey was conducted among approximately 2,020 self-identified U.S. GLBT adult travelers (ages 21 and older) who have taken at least one leisure trip within the past 12 months. In addition, another 1,010 U.S. non-GLBT adult travelers were surveyed. Both populations were drawn from the Harris Poll Online Panel (HPOL). Survey was fielded September 12 through September 21, 2006. Both a nationally stratified random sample and a GLBT over sample were drawn.

The random sample was first weighted to be nationally projectable and used to develop a profile of the GLBT population that was used to weight the GLBT over sample to be nationally projectable. Sexual orientation is defined based on respondents' self-reported identification. Those identifying as bisexual were asked follow up questions about their partner choices (same sex versus opposite sex partners).

The TIA research study set out to research:

- Aided and unaided awareness of destinations that are "gay-friendly"

- The role of "gay-friendly" in overall destination choice

- What "gay friendly" means to this traveler and how a company can take action to make their product gay-friendly

- The most popular types of destinations for gay and lesbian travelers

- The types of vacation plans gay and lesbian travelers would like to make but feel uncomfortable/unwelcome

- Sources of information for trip planning and booking patterns

So what were the most important criteria for a destination to be gay-friendly? They responded in this order of importance:

- "Is generally identified as a place where gay visitors and same-sex couples are known to be safe from harassment, intimidation, threats or physical violence (a place where I can hold my partner's hand in public)"

- "Is a city or community known to be culturally welcoming, and to support diversity and GLBT civil rights"

- "Positive word of mouth from gay friends, relatives and colleagues"

- "Has gay nightlife, gay clubs and/or gay bars"

- "Is located in a state, province or part of a country known to be culturally welcoming and to support diversity and GLBT civil rights"

Among the many highlights of the report, when traveling alone, gay men spent more on their most leisure trip than heterosexuals, $800 compared to $540, respectively. Lesbians spent $570 on their most recent leisure trip while bisexuals in a same-sex relationship spent $690.

A comprehensive report is available for a fee. To purchase a full copy of this report, contact the TIA. Visit tia.org.

"The way in which TIA conducted its 2006 research looks good to me," continues Dr. Diamond. "The difference between the TIA and other gay research that is out there is the sample they are asking gay and straight people the same questions and including general travel information. This has not been done before."

Gay men, lesbians and bisexuals

The travel industry is beginning to recognize that gay men travel differently than lesbians. In general, it was not until 2006 that lesbians began to be more widely recognized as a distinct market within the gay travel market. Compared to gay men, they are interested in different vacations, they consume media differently and they cannot be marketed to just like the boys. Tourism professionals and *Out Traveler* magazine have acknowledged that the next big frontier in gay travel is lesbians. For years, people in the gay travel industry would say that lesbians are too hard to find to research.

The rise in the power of the lesbian market is clearly evident by the very successful Olivia™ which claims the title of the number one lesbian lifestyle company in the world.[18] Olivia has been growing at an extraordinary pace since its founding in San Francisco in 1973. In fact, it is growing beyond cruises to include land vacations and even a credit card. In 2006, MBNA America Bank, N.A., introduced the Olivia Credit Cards. In 2006, Judy Dlucagz, founder and president, and Amy Errett, CEO, won the Ernst and Young Entrepreneur of the Year® 2006 Award in the consumer services category in Northern California. More than anyone else, Olivia knows what lesbians want in travel.

While gay men and lesbians do share similar beliefs and media habits, ongoing primary and secondary research is telling tourism marketers that a slightly different approach is needed when trying to influence lesbians.

In its second gay research study, *Gay Tourism 2005*, the GPTMC became the first destination to dedicate a section solely to lesbian visitors.[19] The study is available for free at gophila.com/research. This first-of-its-kind study revealed that when compared with gay men, lesbian travelers to Philadelphia:

• spend the same per day

• are more likely to be younger

• tend to travel with partners rather than with friends

• are less likely to recall Philly's gay advertising

In addition, gay men are staying longer in Philadelphia (on average 2.4 nights) while lesbians are staying for a shorter period of time (just 1.8 nights).

"Gay Tourism 2005 is significant because the findings challenge many preconceived notions about the economic strength of the lesbian travel segment," said Tom Roth, president of CMI based in San Francisco, California.

The Philadelphia research study also showed that after Provincetown, Massachusetts, there is not a clear top 10 destination list for lesbians, providing a huge opportunity for destinations around the world to fill out that list.

Gay Tourism 2005 also revealed that Philadelphia's website, gophila.com/gay, needed more lesbian-oriented content, which was added that same year. Moreover, while the very successful gay tourism campaign did make lesbians think that Philadelphia was gay-friendly, the advertising didn't specifically speak to them. The very next year, Philadelphia began an aggressive effort to court lesbians, not just through advertising and public relations but also through event sponsorship, including events at the Dinah in Palm Springs, California. Later, we will discuss how to market to lesbians and what makes a destination or a travel product lesbian-friendly.

"Bisexuals are interesting because they represent what may be a potentially sizeable market," said Bob Witeck. "The question that marketers have to ask is what type of relationship is the bisexual in at the time, a same-sex or opposite sex one? If they have a same sex partner at the time and they attend gay events or read gay media or visit gay websites, then you may have a target market. Any marketing to bisexuals perhaps should be focused on the bisexuals who are influenced by gay people and gay media."

> The problem, in my view, is that bisexuality can sometimes be more stigmatized than being gay. If you don't include them, you leave a lot of people out. There are political and cultural issues to overcome. A lot of marketers don't know how to deal with bisexuality.

Gay marriage equals gay dollars

On February 12, 2004, San Francisco's Mayor Newsom announced through the media that he believed that California Constitution allowed for marriage between same-sex couples. The first gay couple to get married was Phyllis Lyon age 79 and Del Martin age 83.[20] Around 4000 other couples also married in San Francisco in that brief period. In February 2004, talk show host and R Family Vacations Founders Rosie O'Donnell married her girlfriend, Kelli Carpenter, with a ceremony in San Francisco Mayor Gavin Newsom's office. Rosie and Kelli have four children together and they were the city's first celebrity gay marriage. On August 12, 2004, the Supreme Court of California ruled that the marriages were void.[21]

Media from all over the world covered this unprecedented event. CMI released a research study that found that gay marriage was a potential financial boom to San Francisco and potentially to other cities that offered same-sex marriage.

On the news of gay weddings starting in San Francisco, CMI initiated a review of tier 2003 market research and its historical trend data to identify the potential economic impact of gay marriage to a destination.

CMI's David Paisley and his partner got married themselves in San Francisco during this extraordinary time. Dave, a local, stood in line with tourists. Some flew red-eye flights and stayed in deluxe hotels while others got in their car and drove. Thousands of people waited for hours for the chance to say those two important words, "I do."

According to CMI, stores located in the Castro, San Francisco's gay neighborhood, reported record-breaking sales and many – from Gold's Gym to restaurants and cafés – promoted "wedding specials" for the just-married. CMI's focus groups and ongoing surveys consistently indicated that gay consumers "vote with their wallets"; they distinctly prefer to visit gay-welcoming destinations and purchase from gay-friendly suppliers when possible. In the 2004 survey, 79 percent indicated that "progressive social policies" are important to them when making their vacation planning decisions, and 93 percent indicated that "feeling welcome and secure" is important.

How big is the gay marriage market? Here is Tom Roth's theory based on 11 years of data: Take the population estimates of GLBT people in the United States, around 15 million, assume that 10 million people are in a committed relationship and a conservative 15 percent of same-gender couples get married, or 1.5 million, and a conservative 15 percent of these couples would travel for a commitment ceremony, the economic impact of the wedding services, honeymoon, and others, and it could grow to nearly $1 billion, or perhaps far more.

The point is that gay commitment ceremonies have the potential to be a huge boon for the travel industry. While some research from CMI shows that in general gay men and lesbians spend significantly less than straight couples do on their wedding, gay commitment ceremonies are a great opportunity to generate business. Increasingly, hotels are beginning to dedicate the sales teams to the gay commitment ceremony market. In addition to human resources, some hotels, including the Mariott Philadelphia, are investing in collateral materials that show gay couples getting hitched.

European gay research

In Europe, Out Now Consulting (www.outnowconsulting.com) is a market leader in gay marketing research and strategy. This company, led by Ian Johnson, holds data on the European sector. Out Now clients include the German National Tourist Office, Qantas Airways, Visit Britain, South African Tourism and others.

The official estimate from the government of the United Kingdom is that 6 percent of the population is gay or lesbian, or 3 million people.[22] Leisure travel features very highly in gay and lesbian spending patterns with total expenditure of more than 3 billion pounds being spent on tourism during 2005.[23] This survey also found that the U.K. gay and lesbian community earns 70 billion pounds annually.

In December 2006, Out Now and Gay Community News (GCN), Ireland's longest running gay national publication, announced a new research study called the Out Now GCN Ireland Gay Market Survey to find out "how green is the pink Euro?" The survey seeks to reveal insights into the lifestyle, opinions and spending patterns on the 200,000 gay and lesbian men living in Ireland.[24] The study's results will be available in 2007.

Nontraditional ways to measure success

Anything that can be measured is always more valued than that which cannot be measured. In gay tourism marketing, there are number of ways to measure the success of a gay tourism campaign. Room nights are key, but also consider measuring clicks to a website, downloads of a gay brochure, revenue per cabin for gay passengers, incidental purchases by known gay hotel guests, participation in affinity program, comments by gay consumers to your guest book, numbers of news articles and word of mouth.

Expert soapbox

Mesearch versus research

Deborah Diamond, Director of Research & Strategy[25]
Greater Philadelphia Tourism Marketing Corporation

I love this term, mesearch versus research. Oftentimes, it is tempting to think that your experience or the experiences of the gay travelers you know is representative of the entire group. This is mesearch. This is very dangerous. While individual perceptions and experiences can be helpful in many ways for your gay tourism marketing efforts, do not rely on this information solely. Not all gay travelers travel alike and that is why research is needed.

Just because you are gay doesn't mean you participate in all these gay niches. Soliciting insight from gay advisors is important, especially if there is no one internally to the company who has access to those perceptions. However, be forewarned that there is generally a difference between the leaders of the gay community and general gay and lesbian consumer. Stakeholders do play an important role in the research process; but the information they hold may not be complete.

The problem with mesearch is that it is subjective. It may be true, but it also may not be true. We have a tendency to believe what we are familiar with than what we are not familiar with. It is dangerous because if it is true for you, it doesn't mean it is the whole story.

You must conduct your own research to learn what is true about your destination and why it may be a good place for gay and lesbian people to visit. In addition to an online research study, you need to recruit a focus group and not just at a gay bar. It is better to go relatively neutral places. The whole point of research is to define as objectively as possible what is true.

What does the future hold for gay research? There will always be gay-focused events and those should be tracked separately. Gay travel is a whole category within travel and it is likely to stay. The question is will gay travel be absorbed into general research or will it become like women business travelers? It is not an oxymoron anymore. There is a possibility that it can be absorbed into everyday marketing including marketing research. There is a strong probability that gay tourism will remain controversial for a really long time in the United States.

Case study

Dallas, Texas and the Dallas Tavern Guild
Creating partnerships between community, government and tourism

Michael Doughman[26]

The Dallas Tavern Guild, a group of member nightclubs that are gay owned and operated, was formed the autumn of 1984 to be

Winners of the 2005 and 2006 Hottest Cowboys Contest, a brilliant promotion for Dallas, Texas. From left to right are real cowboys, winners, Matthew Hey, Matt Shomer, Paul Haynes and Steve Hammond. (Printed with permission from the Dallas Tavern Guild).

the official sponsor and organizing agency for the Dallas Gay Pride Parade. The chief organizer, Alan Ross, was instrumental in developing the parade and other annual events for the gay community.

As the late 1980s brought a crush of conservatism to the Dallas area, several incidents of police harassment were recorded by several clubs. The bar owners quickly learned that the Dallas Tavern Guild brought them a stronger voice because of its number of clubs. Through the guild, they collectively protested the police harassment by showing up repeatedly at city council meetings, writing letters and talking with local merchants in the neighborhood. They complained that the harassment was discrimination based solely on sexuality. The effort paid off when they were able to command the attention of the Dallas Police Department and the City of Dallas. After several months of deliberation and ongoing discussion, they assigned a police sergeant, Sgt. Earl Newsome, to oversee the police patrol in the Oaklawn, Dallas' gay neighborhood. Earl was a straight man with a family but extremely understanding and compassionate of all humanity and the innate rights of all people to be treated equally.

Sgt. Earl Newsome established a significant bridge between the police department and the GLBT community. He implemented sensitivity training for his officers who patrolled the area. This was the very beginning of creating a relationship between the government and the community. The relationship would later evolve into a partnership between the Dallas Police Department and the Dallas GLBT community. Today, there is still an officer dedicated to the GLBT community.

This was the late 1980s and at this time openly gay men and women began running, and were elected, to prominent city offices, including the city council. More lines of communication were established at new levels in government and the relationship improved with the gay community.

The Dallas Tavern Guild continued to manage the parade and to work in developing the Dallas GLBT nightlife, with city support, throughout the 1990s and into the next millennium. However, the guild still lacked the financial resources to grow. Economic independence was essential in order for the guild to function and to grow.

This economic need led to the Dallas Tavern Guild to develop an innovative concept: to approach the most affluent ally the Dallas GLBT community had, the beer and liquor industry.

The Dallas Tavern Guild determined that, collectively, it represented millions of dollars in spirits and beer product purchased each year. It made sense that the guild could leverage the buying power of the GLBT community into some form of reciprocal exchange with the various spirit and beer companies to benefit Dallas. In a nutshell, the GLBT community buys a product; so therefore, we want financial support for our community and our events, especially those events that raised money for people living with HIV and AIDS. Keep in mind that spirit, beer and wine companies support straight events all the time but continue, in most areas of the United States, to ignore the gay community.

The first step was to research the beverage sales and find out exactly how much product the collective membership of the Dallas Tavern Guild, at the time 23 clubs, purchased. These sales figures were combined into monthly, quarterly and annual reports. They were also subdivided into product sales by distributor. The guild learned that the GLBT clubs almost always outsold other mainstream club businesses. Dallas was also, surprisingly, the top market per capita for the beverage industry.

The second step was to tell the membership of the Dallas Tavern Guild the actual dollars they were collectively spending buying spirits, wine and beer. Most knew their own spending figures, but few realized the impact of the collective group.

The final step was to take our information to the distributors and make a proposal to negotiate a partnership. The key objectives for the partnership were as follows:

- Generate more capital for the Dallas Tavern Guild events that would translate into more money given to our annual beneficiaries, which currently number 4–6 each year.
- Create opportunity for the distributors to give their products more exposure and increase sales through club promotions, sponsorship of major community events and marketing.
- Create more business for the member clubs through promotions and support of the various beer and liquor distributors with more consumers buying their product.
- Create a more positive image of both the Dallas Tavern Guild and the beverage industry through community support and participation in benevolent projects.

When this new way of supporting the community was originally proposed, nearly all distributors responded positively and came onboard right away. That was good because if the Dallas Tavern Guild found resistance, its members were committed to removing the product that resisted from its clubs. This was an essential rule if the guild was to find more funding.

In one instance, a liquor company did refuse to participate. A sign was placed in plain view at each cash register in each gay club declaring,

> We currently do not carry "this brand" since the company does not support the GLBT community and the Guild's efforts to raise money for AIDS/HIV service agencies.

Sales immediately plummeted for this brand of liquor while the sales of its competitor brand soared. This bold move had a powerful impact and soon resolved the indifference of the dissenting distributor.

This concept has grown into a highly significant partnership with enormous success for all parties concerned. The community, the Dallas Tavern Guild clubs and the beverage companies have all achieved marked success by building this partnership. The partnerships that the Dallas Tavern Guild developed since first implementing the program has increased the revenues the Dallas Tavern Guild raises, from an initial $5000–$10,000 a year to an amount well over $150,000 annually. Most of this is a cash exchange, but there is also support of in-kind services such as advertising, product, promotional materials and tourism marketing.

Now that this program has matured, the funding does not all come from beer and liquor distributors. As the financial support grew, it enabled the events to grow in scale and quality, resulting in more companies and businesses approaching the Dallas Tavern Guild to become partners in our community events.

The result is this clear: nearly all of Dallas' annual gay events are completely underwritten. This gives us the chance to give more to our beneficiaries, to create bigger and better events and to develop tourism programs to promote the GLBT community in Dallas. An example of a beneficiary program is a beautification project for the Oaklawn neighborhood and the resident gathering place, Lee Park, which hosts multiple GLBT functions.

Most importantly, the funding has attained a much higher level of respect for the nightclub business in the Dallas community and our partners in the beverage industry have each seen significant increases in sales and visibility of product. It also links both the nightclubs and the liquor companies to many positive, community-oriented projects each year.

Within five years, what was an innovative funding idea for gay events eventually allowed the guild to develop a great partnership with the Dallas Convention and Visitors Bureau (CVB). I knew that Dallas needed to be an active force in the GLBT destinations in the United States. But, I didn't really know how many great resources and people there were to help me make that vision happen until I attended the CMI's International Gay and Lesbian Tourism Conference in 2003. There I met many leaders in gay tourism, including Jeff Guaracino, and found the resources that would put Dallas on the map as a top gay and lesbian tourism destination.

Soon after the conference and with the funding from the guild, we were able to underwrite most of the expenses for the first GLBT media familiarization trip to Dallas. Now, annually, the guild still contributes to the cost of bringing journalists here. In addition to the press trips, we worked with the Dallas CVB to extend the mainstream tourism marketing from the Dallas CVB into the GLBT market. We applied traditional marketing strategies for selling a destination but remolded the images to feature the strengths and attributes of the GLBT community. We wanted the diversity marketing to be specific and appealing without feeling too separate from the mainstream tourism message as not to make the GLBT market feel marginalized.

The Dallas gay marketing features, what else, cowboys. Why cowboys? In talking to gay and lesbian folks from all over the country and the world, I always asked what would be the most appealing fantasy of going to Dallas. Most said it would be meeting a real cowboy or cowgirl. That made it obvious that although Dallas had much, much more to offer than just cowboys, it is still an intriguing and appealing mental image and we couldn't overlook them as a genuine attraction for Dallas. Other destinations have beaches, ski resorts or Disney, but we have hot cowboys and beautiful cowgirls.

In 2006, *USA Today* did a cover story on destinations in Red States that are marketing themselves as gay-friendly tourism spots. It certainly wasn't easy to launch a gay tourism campaign in George Bush's backyard, but we believe that a very powerful tool in selling Dallas, or any place for that matter, as a gay-friendly destination is to show financial credibility and grassroots support that comes from the GLBT community. Therefore, the guild is prominent in our GLBT tourism marketing outreach. Our community support supersedes local politics. Yes, Dallas happens to be located in a Red State and we are still a great place for the GLBT community to visit.

The guild and local GLBT leaders continue to work in partnership with the Dallas CVB for ongoing education about gay and lesbian travelers. Gay people play an active role in the Diversity Marketing Committee and serve on the Dallas CVB Board of Directors. The Dallas CVB invites GLBT leaders to participate in developing future marketing strategies for this market including gay consumer expos, gay meetings and conventions and gay sporting events.

The Dallas Tavern Guild model is a model that has real application capabilities for almost any city. It is already showing success in Philadelphia and is currently in development for several other cities across the country.

Alan, the man who started the guild, died in 1995 and the parade was officially named in his honor. In 2008, the Alan Ross Texas Freedom Parade will celebrate its 25th anniversary.

Notes

1. Gay Tourism 2003, Greater Philadelphia Tourism Marketing Corporation, Community Marketing Inc., November 2003.
2. Diamond, Deborah, Ph.D., in-person interview, August 14, 2006.
3. Diamond, Deborah, Ph.D., in-person interview, August 14, 2006.
4. U.S. Census (2000), Witeck–Combs/Harris Interactive (2000–2003), Kaiser Family Foundation (2002).
5. U.S. Census (2000).
6. The U.S. Gay and Lesbian Market, Fourth Edition, 2006, Witeck–Combs and Packaged Facts.

7. Selig Center for Economic Growth, University of Georgia, U.S. Census projections (2005) and U.S. Bureau of Economic Affairs.
8. Witeck, Robert, in-person interview, October 15, 2005.
9. Gay and Lesbian Tourism Profile 2006, October 2006, Community Marketing, Inc., San Francisco, CA.
10. Gay and Lesbian Tourism Profile 2006, October 2006, Community Marketing, Inc., San Francisco, CA.
11. Gay and Lesbian Tourism Profile 2006, October 2006, Community Marketing, Inc., San Francisco, CA.
12. Gay and Lesbian Tourism Profile 2006, October 2006, Community Marketing, Inc., San Francisco, CA.
13. Gay and Lesbian Tourism Profile 2006, October 2006, Community Marketing, Inc., San Francisco, CA.
14. Gay and Lesbian Tourism Profile 2006, October 2006, Community Marketing, Inc., San Francisco, CA.
15. Gay and Lesbian Tourism Profile 2006, October 2006, Community Marketing, Inc., San Francisco, CA.
16. Cooke, Dr. Suzanne, Traveler's Use of the Internet 2005, Travel Industry of America.
17. Travel Industry of America.
18. Olivia, www.olivia.com, September 2006, San Francisco, CA.
19. *Gay Tourism 2005*, March 2005, Greater Philadelphia Tourism Marketing Corporation, Community Marketing Inc.
20. Gordon, Andrew, Green Deatherage, Sherri, Weddings in San Francisco Give PR Boost to Gay Unions, *PR Week*, February 23, 2004.
21. Whitehall, December 2005.
22. Whitehall, December 2005.
23. Out Now Consulting, 2005, Gay Times and Diva Readers Survey, United Kingdom.
24. Out Now Consulting, 2007, GCN Ireland Gay Market Survey, United Kingdom.
25. Diamond, Deborah, Ph.D., in-person interview, August 14, 2006.
26. Doughman, Michael, interviews, submitted copy to author, June 2006.

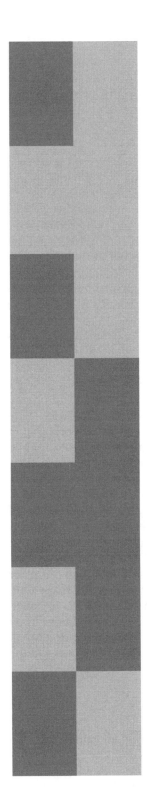

Building stakeholder support: don't go it alone

The key to any successful gay tourism initiative, no matter how small or large, is to engage both your GLBT stakeholders and straight stakeholders. For destinations, this means your local gay community, and for companies, this means your gay employees and customers.

Your goal is to build support and understanding for your effort among all groups. Your strategy must ensure that your likely allies understand where you are going, why you are doing it and how it is going to be done. Building support for your effort whether in the boardroom, among employees or with the community does not happen overnight. Stakeholder support is built over time and built with trust and mutual understanding of the end goal. Building support is never finished. It is always reaffirmed and reassured.

With gay tourism, there are many questions upfront that you will need to answer for your stakeholders. Often, people will bring up political or religious objections. I have been asked, isn't gay sex immoral? I have also been asked about stereotypes that are mistaken for truths. I have been asked why should we market to lesbians, they don't spend money, do they? Another common question is why can't there just be one campaign that speaks to everyone? For anyone who pays close attention to the vanishing mass market and who realizes that, in reality, the minority markets are the new majority, it is easy to understand why one size does not fit all.

Too often, there is a gap between the GLBT community and the tourism office. This is a mistake. You must engage your local GLBT community or your GLBT employees in the effort. In some destinations, the local business community created its own gay tourism marketing efforts long before receiving official support from the destination marketing organization. In others, the tourism office was first when it came to promoting the destination as gay-friendly before there was strong community involvement. It is the chicken versus the egg argument, sometimes one has to come first and you never know which group will be first to raise their hand. The very best model is when the tourism agency works in partnership with the local gay community, as in the case of Bloomington, Indiana, Fort Lauderdale, Florida, and Philadelphia.

For other companies in tourism, the best scenario is to work together with an expert in the gay market, whether it is a gay tour operator, as in the case of Royal Caribbean Cruise Line and Atlantis Events, or it is a marketing firm that specializes in GLBT tourism. Perhaps, American Airlines is the best example of a company working with its gay employees to guide their company successfully in the gay tourism marketplace.

Take caution though and define early the role that each of your stakeholders will play to support your effort. Rarely will the stakeholder group that you will bring together be experts in tourism or your product. You are the tourism expert. You have the product knowledge and you have the resources to shine a spotlight on a particular community, an annual gay event or something special about the place you are going to be marketing. The people in the GLBT community are often experts in something other than tourism. They are small business owners. They are social activists. They are newspaper publishers or festival producers. These people are the product, the influencers and the doers.

Why do you need stakeholder support?

First and foremost, you want your gay tourism campaign to be successful! You want to promote an authentic product and you want to be sure that you can deliver on the marketing promise.

You also need to better understand if the product that you are promoting is already gay visitor ready or if you need to develop tourism product, as in the case of Bloomington, Indiana, when they began to support the GLBT film festival. Another example of how your stakeholder groups can make the product better is when gay tour operators charter mainstream cruise ships. The cruise lines have wonderful entertainment and amenities; however, gay tour operators have educated the cruise lines on how and what they need to do to make an all-gay cruise vacation a better experience for the gay traveler.

Getting started

"The first question you should ask is who might this impact positively and negatively?," said Meryl Levitz, president and CEO of Greater Philadelphia Tourism Marketing Corporation.[1] She suggests that the first step is to create a mental list of who might be with you, who might be against you and who might be hurt by a gay tourism program?

"For Philadelphia, we spent a year to do research and to establish a baseline of support," said Levitz. "You don't want to be in a position of one day looking behind you and not seeing anyone there following you to the goal."

Who are your stakeholder groups? They are as follows:

Elected officials including city council, the mayor and governor

State and regional tourism agencies, CVBs and their members

Employees, executive staff and board of your organization

Journalists and news organizations

Gay event and festival producers

Organized business, civic and cultural associations

GLBT community at large

Gay chambers of commerce, if your city has one

Straight community at large

Accommodations including hotels and B&Bs

The visitor center

Restaurants, shops and nightclubs (both gay and straight)

Anyone that has a stake in what you are doing, especially those who fund your organization

Do you have to be gay?

I remember the day that Sharon Rossi, vice president of advertising, at GPTMC asked me the question, "Do you have to be gay to be involved in the Philadelphia Gay Tourism Caucus?" I was surprised by her question. I had never considered that my straight colleagues would think that the Caucus was not for them. I had always thought it was obvious. Yes, we need straight allies.

Building stakeholder support should not be limited to the gay community. What a big mistake! While you will find that the gay community will be the most active and informed members of the stakeholder group, it is essential to keep your straight allies informed of your progress. Oftentimes, you will find that the straight allies in the stakeholder groups welcome the opportunity to participate in and to support the effort but they need a path to follow. What they really need are ways to become a part of the gay tourism program that fits within their own business model.

Tips for building stakeholder support

This is a multistep approach. First, create an advisory committee that is mainly focused on tourism initiatives, and second, develop an educational program for the stakeholders that you have identified.

The first step is to get the right people around a table. Are they a good cross-section of the community at large? Is there diverse representation from the aforementioned list? Try to be inclusive. Invite everyone to the table. Eventually, the group may self-select and the most committed people will come back and participate. Others may want periodic updates. The important thing here is that everyone has an opportunity to participate.

The second step is to identify a group facilitator. In general, it is best to choose someone who is relatively neutral. This role can be played by anyone and, if possible but not mandatory, a gay person with strong relationships within the local community. You need someone to lead the effort. You need an organized person who will set an agenda, who will keep the discussion on track and who gives everyone equal opportunity to express an opinion. The committee needs a mission statement and a set of goals. Consider developing a collaborative gay marketing plan that incorporates marketing, product development and education.

Third, educate everyone! To be honest, there are no fast and easy rules. However, there are techniques that you can utilize that will facilitate your goals. Begin by educating the local stakeholder group with tourism facts. They should be aware of the economic benefits of gay tourism and the discussion should not be focused on political, social or religious issues. Clearly explain what you are attempting to achieve and why you are going to engage in a tourism campaign. Furthermore, openly discuss stereotypes and create an atmosphere where people's concerns, fears or misconceptions can be resolved. Do not tolerate homophobia.

Empower your most connected supporters to be vocal. Multiple voices lend credibility to the effort. Also, different people have different spheres of influence, so it is important to encourage people to talk about what you are doing and why. Be sure that everyone keeps the key message points consistent.

Set a larger purpose for the group. The group you convene should have specific goals and tactics but the members of the group themselves should develop the strategy to achieve the goals. A goal is not just to launch a gay tourism campaign. Yes that is true, but perhaps goals are to write and produce a gay brochure, to develop a list of gay groups and conventions that can bring business to the destination or perhaps to organize a host committee to bring gay sporting competitions to an area. Once group members see the results of their work, they usually will remain very motivated.

Finally, set regular meeting times. This is essential to ensure consistency and buy-in. People need to meet at scheduled intervals so the effort gains momentum. Sometimes groups choose to have their own identity, separate from the destination marketer or within the company. For example, in Fort Lauderdale they created an independent logo and a name for their group. While seemingly insignificant, giving this effort a unique name gives this group a sense of identity.

Another valuable tip from Ms. Levitz is to bring your creative concepts, timelines and media plans to all your relevant stakeholders, starting with your board, to show what you are doing and why it is important and strategic. Depending on your company or destination, it may include your mayor or governor or perhaps your CEO or shareholders.

"During the time that Philadelphia was building our support base, we chose the right agency and conduct our research so that we could be ready to take aim and then fire," Meryl continued.

> GPTMC learned a lot while we were building our support. We first asked why would people believe us that Philadelphia is gay-friendly? We also learned from our stakeholder group what our destination's strength's and weakness' were so we could develop a campaign that would not over promise and under deliver. We made sure that we had a product and that somebody wanted

it. At the same time we were able to tap into the political resources of the local gay community and that was an immediate plus. During this phase we also earned the support of the hoteliers and retailers.

What about backlash?

During this process, it is inevitable that, someone somewhere will be against you. The trick is to have enough people who support you. It is a right to advertise to the GLBT Community not a liability. A true turning point for the advertising community in the United States occurred on April 3, 2006, when the industry collectively stood up against conservative groups, such as the American Family Association, that threatened boycotts anytime a company launched a marketing campaign toward the gay consumer. An editorial in *Advertising Age* said it all with the headline, "A vote against discrimination".[2]

The editorial said,

> We commend the Association of National Advertisers and the American Association of Advertising Agencies for endorsing the right of marketers to target gay consumers. This is good business. It's also a strong reminder that discrimination and intolerance are not the American way. The ANA and 4A's singed on as supporters of the Principle of Free Market Advertising Expression, conceived by the Commercial Closet, a gay-advocacy group.

Respected public relations firm Fleishman-Hillard and its internal gay practice group, FH Out Front, sponsored a national consumer survey in 2004 that demonstrates that companies need not be overly concerned about backlash or boycotts as a result of targeting this important brand-loyal audience.[3] The FH Out Front Survey found that reaching out to GLBT audiences does not negatively impact at large consumer perceptions of a company or its products.

- Sixty-eight percent indicate that knowing a company promotes its products or services to gays and lesbians has no effect on how they feel about the company.

- Eighty-one percent indicate that it does not matter to them if a company whose products they use on a regular basis also promotes those products to the gay and lesbian community.

Boycotts against GLBT-related opposition draw twice as much opposition to the boycotters as they do to the targeted company:

- Eight percent of respondents would participate
- Twenty percent of respondents would speak out against the boycott
- Forty-six percent of respondents would do nothing

There is so much more to say on this subject of blacklash and this entire book is dedicated to the very best practices. As Nike says, Just Do It! If you are not, the rest of the world is and is enjoying your fair share of the economic pie.

Case study

When the gay hits the fan, and it did!

There are plenty of reasons why you need stakeholder support. Let me tell you a story that happened in Philadelphia that showed how broad-based stakeholder support played itself out and why it is so important to have allies who speak for you.

On June 9, 2005, Pennsylvania State Representative Daryl D. Metcalfe wrote a memo address to all members of the House of Representatives in the Commonwealth of Pennsylvania. It was also subsequently distributed to nearly every lobbyist as well.[4] He wrote,

> It has been brought to my attention by one of my concerned constituents that our tax dollars are being used to promote immoral behaviors! Attached you will find a copy of the information that Philadelphia is using to promote "tourism" within the city. My constituents, as well as a majority of Pennsylvanians across this great Commonwealth, consider this as funding an offensive behavior with which they disagree!

As you can imagine, this memo certainly caused a firestorm of gossip in Harrisburg, Pennsylvania. To make matters worse, it was the height of the budget season, so millions of dollars of tourism funding could have been at stake.

To the rescue came Representative James R. Roebuck.[5] On June 16, 2005, he countered the memo by saying,

Recently Representative Daryl Metcalfe circulated a memorandum to members of the House asserting that Philadelphia is using our tax dollars to promote immoral behaviors. He cites various state grants which he asserts where used to promote gay tourism to the City. Representative Metcalfe's assertions, however, are wrong. No tax dollars were used to underwrite the tourism promotion to which he objects. The initiative is supported by dollars from the hotel industry. These business people believe it is important to go after a market which returns significant dollars to the city and to the Commonwealth. The campaign is not a political or social statement. Every dollar spent on media returns $185 to the Commonwealth plus $13 in state and local taxes. It is good business. While Representative Metcalfe might want to raise objections to the effort, he should have his facts straight.

This memo to all of the PA House of Representatives prompted yet another rebuttal memo from Representative Metcalfe.[6] He wrote,

I would like to clarify some statements made by Representative James Roebuck ... GPTMC is responsible for producing the 30-second television commercial to promote its 'Get Your History Straight and Your Nightlife Gay' advertising campaign. Representative Roebuck asserts that the gay tourism initiative is supported by dollars from the hotel industry ... however ... 33 percent of its funding comes from the Commonwealth of Pennsylvania in a form of appropriations or grants. Thus ... state tax dollars are still being used to offset other administrative, media and research, which in turn allows this controversial program to be funded by the hotel industry money. In closing, I stand by my argument that a majority of Pennsylvanians do not support funding tourism promotion aimed at a lifestyle choice that is against their religious and moral beliefs.

It didn't take long for these memos to be leaked to a journalist. On Monday, June 27, 2005,[7] the media firestorm blazed out of control. The headline in *The Philadelphia Inquirer* read: Memo blasts funding to attract gay tourists. In this story, Metcalfe defended his memos by saying he thinks homosexuality is immoral. Roebuck countered saying what is offensive is not a particular group's sexual preference but the discrimination against any group of people. Meryl Levitz, GPTMC president and CEO, said, "Philadelphia and Pennsylvania were founded on welcoming all people. To try and punish an organization for extending a welcome that really bothers me because that is not what Philadelphia and Pennsylvania are all about." Malcolm Lazin, prominent gay community member and founder of Equality Forum, an annual international gay event held in Philadelphia, said, "This is what I call nasty and divisive politics."

The Philadelphia Inquirer article was not the last. Sandy Shea at the *Philadelphia Daily News* wrote an editorial on June 29, 2005, with the headline "Macho Man" that took a direct slam at Representative Metcalfe.[8] On Monday, July 11th, *The Philadelphia Inquirer* wrote an editorial that lead with this headline, "Gay or straight; who cares?" Even the general public became engaged in the debate and wrote letters to the editor to support GPTMC and vent their anger at Metcalfe. This debate continued until the end of July.

MONDAY
JULY 11, 2005

The Philadelphia Inquirer

50¢
75 cents in some locations outside the metropolitan area

City & Suburbs Edition   c   W W W . P H I L L Y . C O M   177th Year No. 41

Seeking Tourists With Cash

Gay or straight; who cares?

The primary job of the Greater Philadelphia Tourism Marketing Corp. is to attract large groups of tourists who will drop buckets of cash in the region. So it makes sense for it to team with groups promoting niche tourism markets, including the Equality Forum, a nonprofit dedicated to equality for gays and lesbians.

Enter state Rep. Daryl D. Metcalfe (R., Butler), who during the recent legislative session sent letters to House members in which he wailed against using public dollars "to fund behavior that is against their religious and moral beliefs."

GPTMC does receive some state money, which it says is used mostly for operational expenses. Much of its marketing funds come from a regional hotel tax. But where the

cash goes is almost is beside the point when considering Metcalfe's homophobic remarks.

The tourism agency isn't spending money to encourage any type of "behavior." It's simply trying to lure tourists from all walks of life who have disposable income to spend. A GPTMC study shows the region received $153 in direct spending by gay visitors for every dollar spent on ads that targeted gay tourists.

Malcolm Lazin, executive director of the Equality Forum, says GPTMC has followed a smart business plan based on studies that show gay and lesbian travelers represent a $50 billion-a-year tourism market.

Philadelphia has a dozen other tourism campaigns aimed at niche markets, including ethnic,

professional and business groups.

"We'd be irresponsible if we didn't market to the gay market," says GPTMC president Meryl Levitz. Hotel chains, travel agencies, airlines, even countries, including Canada and Mexico, are targeting gay tourists.

If he studied, Metcalfe might learn that many cities have been revived by gay residents whose typically higher incomes allow investments in pricey residential properties that yield significant local tax revenue.

States with smart leaders are benefiting from the positive economic impact that gay residents can bring. States with intolerant, tunnel-vision leadership are instead stuck in the mud. Pennsylvania will fit the latter profile if Metcalfe is its guide.

Editorials from *The Philadelphia Inquirer* (Permission to reprint by Philadelphia Newspapers, Inc.)

It was only a matter of time before it hit the press. Local media were supportive of the gay campaign because they understood the goals and additional local allies were found in the local members of NLGJA. These years of building support among media resulted in stories that were sensitive to the gay community and were well balanced and informed.

Furthermore, members of the Philadelphia Gay Tourism Caucus (PGTC), including Philadelphia Gay News Publisher Mark Segal, immediately began to contact politicians saying that they support the gay tourism campaign and that this was a hateful attack on GPTMC and the gay community.

There was support from the hotels, the GPTMC Board and even the general public who agreed with the campaign because they too understood the goals. Having other people support and defend the effort from attack was the ideal position to be in.

In the end, the effort did not impact the budget of GPTMC. Matthew Link, editor of *The Out Traveler*, heard of our plight and he wrote a story for the magazine personally. The goal was to educate the travel industry and travelers that while Philadelphia was under attack, gay travelers won![9]

Case study

The Philadelphia Gay Tourism Caucus

Margaret Mede once said, "Never underestimate the power of a small group of people to change the world." She was right. In August 2002, eight people joined together in the boardroom of the Westin Hotel in Philadelphia to have a simple discussion about gay and lesbian travel. Here's how it all started.

John Cochie, Innkeeper of Philadelphia's gay owned and operated Alexander Inn Hotel, was in Fort Lauderdale, Florida for an International Gay and Lesbian Travel Association convention. He was inspired by the wonderful headway Richard Grey, Francine Mason and Nikki Grossman had made in transforming Fort Lauderdale from a Spring Break town to a gay-friendly town. John called me and asked if we could set up a meeting with the key gay community leaders to discuss if Philadelphia could come out as a gay-friendly destination.

By the second meeting, there was a virtual who's who of the gay community including Dan Contarino, Thom Cardwell, Ron Cartieri, John Cochie, Robert DiGiacomo, Mel Heifetz, David Jefferys, Malcolm Lazin, Mickey Rowley, Dave Rumsey, Mark Segal, Mark Chumley Singer, Royal Tettemer, Keith Toler and

Patrice Walsh. No one quite knew what the outcome would be, but this group made just one decision for the first three months: to keep meeting again.

Well, for the next two months, the group in general would complain about what is wrong with the gay community and how, in the past, several good ideas died on the vine, including a past gay tourism effort back in the 1990s. Skepticism threatened to derail the whole idea. The difference with this group, which had no name at this time, was that all of the key decision makers were at the table and they believed that we, the collective we, could do this. We decided that now was the right time and we were the right people. The magic of this particular group of men and women was that everyone brought something different to the table. Some members at the table had access to financial resources while others had political access. Everyone was welcomed.

At the third meeting, we named ourselves the Philadelphia Gay Tourism Caucus, an all-volunteer group with no paid staff. We would all be volunteers and with no paid staff. John Cochie would preside over these meetings for the next two years. As the "elected facilitator", as we called him, he had no additional power, but he was a man whom everyone respected and would set the agenda, write the minutes and facilitate the discussion.

The PGTC had just three rules and they were simple:

1. Anyone and everyone, gay or straight, is invited to participate in the discussion

2. You must bring resources to the effort, whether it be human or financial

3. You must be willing to collaborate and partner with each other

Our first agendas were very simple. We discussed great big ideas and they were very helpful in guiding our discussion. We decided that we needed a common project, a marketing plan. We began to develop our goals and strategies and tactics, which helped us to organize our meeting, kept the discussion focused on tourism and prioritized our ideas.

We immediately began to evaluate what makes Philadelphia a gay-friendly destination. We developed a calendar of events and we began to collect data on how much money was being spent individually by the hotels, by gay event producers and by the GPTMC and the Philadelphia Convention & Visitors Bureau on gay marketing. We were stunned to learn that our individual members were already spending a stunning $200,000 a year in marketing to the gay and lesbian consumer but it was not coordinated – there was no single call to action, no brand development and there were disconnects between the hotels, the events and the tourism agencies.

The PGTC immediately made a strategic decision that was ultimately the key to its long-term success. That decision was to break into subcommittees related to someone's employment, such as the hotel, marketing, event or finance.

Remember, everyone brought something to the table. The Philadelphia CVB created a two-panel brochure that would eventually become a 50-page, four-color gay trip planner. Dave Jeffries, Tami Sortman and the gang at the Altus Group donated their time and services to create Philadelphia Gay Tourism Caucus letterhead and business cards.

Almost a year after the Caucus first met, GPTMC announced a three-year, $1 million gay tourism marketing campaign. GPTMC commissioned a research study through the industry's leading expert, Community Marketing Incorporated. With all these invaluable resources, it would be impossible to measure the creativity, the talent, the political connections and the experience that all the members brought to the table in helping to create Philadelphia's gay-friendly tourism program.

There were times when the Caucus would wrestle with consensus. We knew we wanted the PGTC to have longevity and to live on past the tenures of our original founding members. While it took nearly a year of what seemed like endless discussion, we decided to ask an attorney to create a nonprofit organization with an elected board, bylaws and financial statements. In hindsight, I think that waiting so long was probably a mistake, we should have done it sooner. Yet, I also argue that this group needed time to mature, to get to know each other and to really make sure we wanted the legal responsibility of giving birth to a new organization. The timing was absolutely right, we became a nonprofit in 2005, three years after we first met.

Empowering the PGTC to create and own, operate and manage its own programs was instrumental in bringing about its long-term success. The PGTC, with a $5000 grant from the Center City District approved by Paul Levy and Michelle Shannon, was able to create the nation's best and most organized Gay Friendly Merchant Initiative. The Caucus identified gay-owned and gay-friendly businesses. The Caucus designed a brochure that was distributed to hotel guests who were staying in Caucus member hotels. The brochure is also available at the Independence Visitor Center. In 2006, the Caucus created its second edition of the Gay Friendly Merchant Initiative. This time, Enterprise Rent-A-Car joined the Center City District as financial sponsors. Now a PDF of the brochure is available online at gophila.com.

The 2006 Board of Directors, The Philadelphia Gay Tourism Caucus (Courtesy, The Greater Philadelphia Tourism Marketing Corporation).

In an effort to measure the marketing efforts, the PGTC hotel committee created the Philadelphia Freedom Hotel Package. The hotel package was a product that a gay consumer could buy. In the first year, just 13 hotels offered the package, in the second year, more than 33 hotels, and in the third year, it was back to around 16 hotels. There are many reasons for this. The Caucus solicited the hotels, created the offer and asked GPTMC to sell the package on its website at gophila.com/gay.

By traditional measurements, the hotel package was not a huge success, but it accomplished a very big thing because it was created and managed by the Caucus. However, this is not a failure by any measurement. It is a really "out" traveler who goes online at gophila.com/gay, books a gay hotel package, walks into a hotel and says "I want my gay welcome kit!" So, where did all these gay travelers sleep over? Everywhere they have frequent traveler accounts, in rooms that they booked at a third-party website like Orbitz, the hotels' own website or if they came for a special event like Equality Forum, they brought the Equality Forum Hotel Package.

Another initiative of the PGTC is the "Gayborhood" signage program. New York has Chelsea, Montreal has the Village, San Francisco has the Castro and Philadelphia has the Gayborhood. Led by Chumley Singer, Tami Sortman, Michael Hinson and the Mayor of Philadelphia, the Honorable John F. Street, Philadelphia's 36 rainbow signs were dedicated in April 2007.

While it did take some meetings with community and neighborhood associations, every impacted group approved the Caucus' request to add rainbow decals to street signs located within downtown Philadelphia known by locals as the Gayborhood.

The PGTC continues to meet monthly in executive meetings and conducts a public meeting every other month. The Caucus is now seeking funding to hire an executive director to take the organization to a new level. The Caucus has a dedicated board, supporters and membership that makes it the very best example of tourism and community working together.

Notes

1. Levitz, Meryl, Greater Philadelphia Tourism Marketing Corporation, interview, September 5, 2006.
2. Editorial, A Vote Against Discrimination, *Advertising Age*, April 3, 2006.
3. Fleishman-Hillard, FH Out Front Survey, 2004.
4. Metcalfe, Daryl D., Representative, Commonwealth of Pennsylvania, Philadelphia Tourism Promotion, memo, June 9, 2005.
5. Roebuck, James R., Representative, Commonwealth of Pennsylvania, Philadelphia Tourism Promotion, memo, June 16, 2005.
6. Metcalfe, Daryl D., Representative, Commonwealth of Pennsylvania, Philadelphia Tourism Promotion, memo, June 21, 2005.
7. Couloumbis, Angela, Memo Blasts Funding to Attract Gay Tourists, *The Philadelphia Inquirer*, June 27, 2005.
8. Shea, Sandy, Macho Man, *Philadelphia Daily News*, June 29, 2005.
9. *The Out Traveler*, Fall 2005.

CHAPTER 5

Best practices in gay and lesbian tourism marketing

Shouldn't advertising convey respect instead of perpetuating stereotypes, homophobia and transphobia?

Mike Wilke, founding executive director,
The Commercial Closet

Mike Wilke is a pioneer in advertising. He recognized long before anyone else on Madison Avenue that companies and destinations will have to incorporate gays and lesbians into their overall brand. Sometimes they have done it well and sometimes, they've missed the mark.

In 2005, 175 Fortune 500 companies including airlines, automakers, financial firms and retailers wooed the gay consumer through advertising compared with just 19 in 1994.[1]

The big question facing all of us is, how do you incorporate the gay marketing message into our overall brand? According to Sharon Rossi, vice president of advertising at the Greater Philadelphia Tourism Marketing Corporation, "The first thing you must do is research, as with all niche markets but most especially the gay market because of the increased sensitivity".[2]

"What we know is that the gay traveler is spending twice as much as the mainstream traveler but all that means is that you have to be twice as smart in how you incorporate the gay market into other marketing efforts if you are to gain the largest market share," she continued.

The danger is that you if you create a marketing campaign that is distant from what the consumer already perceives is true about your destination, you will not be successful. Would anyone believe that men are walking around Philadelphia with their shirts off all winter long? Of course not! However, they would believe that Philadelphia has history and they *could* believe that the city had a gay nightlife, even if they had not experienced it for themselves first-hand. Would anyone believe that Royal Caribbean cruises always had ships filled with gays and lesbians? No, but they could believe that the cruise line is filled with lots of active things to do and that the ship's staff are gay-friendly.

"In some ways, it is much easier to do niche market compared to mass marketing but increasingly with any niche market, the message needs to be specific to the consumer while supporting the general campaign," continued Rossi. "That doesn't mean you can not run simultaneous marketing campaigns, one for the mainstream consumer and one for the gay consumer. I think the key in niche marketing is that the message has to be very specific to be heard."

Today, it is the Web that brings all marketing and media relations campaigns together. The Web site is the connector. Marketing should entice consumers to visit the Web site so they can learn everything about your product or service. Smart tourism marketers simply use advertising as a tease to grab the consumer's attention, drive them to go online and then "woo" the consumer. Once they are online, the consumers explore their gay interests and also view everything that the product has to offer. This also answers the questions posed in the research chapter. When is a gay traveler a gay traveler? Sometimes a gay traveler is interested in either outdoor activities or American history, and it doesn't matter if the experience is specifically a gay experience. The web allows marketers to say so much more.

What makes the print creative successful?

This is simple. Get the very best creative talent you can find. Most importantly, he or she doesn't have to be gay or lesbian but has to be armed with research and be in tuned to with the gay market. You must allow your creative person to tailor a message and an image that is true to your destination or travel product. Humor goes a very long way, especially in the gay market. The creative should be attractive, upscale, gay-specific but it should also avoid stereotyping.

Can you use generic advertising creative? sometimes yes and sometimes no. If you do use general market creative, it is very safe but not very courageous. Worse than being perceived as safe, it has the potential to be received by your audience as cheap and interpreted as insulting. You must invest in gay creative, and you want to be respectful. You don't have to scream gay but you have to do it right.

"Companies create gay-themed print advertising because even today there is so little imagery of gay men and women in ads that it stands out dramatically," said Wilke. "Further, the gay community so rarely sees itself reflected in advertising and an ad portraying the group it targets will usually do better than one that does not".[3]

In gay tourism marketing, a picture is still worth a thousand words. Fast forward to 2006 and you will routinely find gay people touching, kissing or embracing in print media. You may even see them in romantic situations, such as the Hyatt Resorts ad with two attractive men under the waterfall. It is amazing how quickly marketers understood that gay and lesbian travelers do want to see themselves enjoying all the aspects of travel fantasy.

Gay codes in advertising

What is gay code? Gay codes are names or symbols that convey that you are gay-friendly without using those exact words. What are some examples of gay code? A rainbow flag, a pink triangle, the Human Rights Campaign logo (an "=" sign within a rectangular blue box), a red AIDS ribbon, a Lambda symbol, the symbol of female or male sexuality with two used together joined at the rings and even the names of famous gay and lesbian events such as the Winter Party in Miami. Astute gay and lesbian travelers will recognize these codes and understand that it is intended to communicate your gay-friendliness. The upside of codes is that, in general, they tend to not alienate other customers who may not notice these or understand their meaning.

Ben Franklin flies a rainbow kite (Courtesy of Greater Philadelphia Tourism Marketing Corporation).

"The gay events you sponsor and your company is involved in sends a signal to your intended audience," said LoAnn Holden.[4] "If you promote on your web site in your advertising that your company is the sponsor of a gay event, let's say the White Party in Miami, a straight person from the Midwest is not going to know that it is a gay event. You will not alienate straight people but a gay person is going to look at it and see that you support gay events. That is also gay code."

"The rainbow flag is overdone," said Tom Roth. "In the future you will see more advertising with text at the bottom of the ad that indicates the company is a supporter of a GLBT community event or a GLBT cause".[5]

Betsy Ross sews a rainbow flag (Courtesy of Greater Philadelphia Tourism Marketing Corporation).

The world's first gay travel television commercials (there are just four!)

Jeff Marsh, formerly of Ortiz and now head of Marsh Partners based in Chicago, said in an August 1, 2003, USA Today interview with Jayne Clark, "Going on TV is the ultimate sign that you're a gay-friendly company".[6]

Orbitz announced on June 9, 2003, the launch of the company's first-ever gay travel television commercial. Orbitz would become the first mainstream travel company to advertise with a gay

"Penn Pals", first television commercial by a destination (Courtesy of Greater Philadelphia Tourism Marketing Corporation).

Nipple boy (2003–2006) (Courtesy of Greater Fort Lauderdale Convention & Visitors Bureau).

specific television commercial. The ad made its debut on Bravo and BBC America during the third week in June to coincide with Pride Month.

The 30-second commercial was a brilliant example of extending the mainstream commercials into the gay market. The gay themed television commercial used the same "Destination: Orbitz" cast of sophisticated marionettes that debuted two months earlier, April 2003. The new gay commercial, which ran for three months, featured the Destination Orbitz Team helping a group of travelers book a hotel room for a long weekend getaway in Miami. At the same time, Orbitz was advertising in

Rainbow Vespa (November 2006–2007) (Courtesy of Greater Fort Lauderdale Convention & Visitors Bureau).

national gay magazines including Advocate, Out and Passport. The company's call to action was www.orbitz.com/gaytravel.[7]

Orbitz was not the first to create and broadcast a television commercial for the gay travel market. That crown is held by Olivia Cruises. In 1997, Olivia Cruises became the first lesbian travel product ever to be advertised on television. According to the Commercial Closet Web, the television spot featured two model-like women on a cruise ship, living the high life. One splashes the other as she tans by the pool, then later gives her a rose. They relax in beach chairs and join each other at the

Women on Bike (Courtesy of Key West).

back of the ship for a private meal served by a waiter. The end shot explains that Olivia provides "vacations for women".[8]

At first glance, you might think it would be easy for Olivia to air their gay television commercial on network television. When the ABC sitcom character, Ellen, on the show "Ellen" and the network refused to air the Olivia commercial, The National Gay and Lesbian Task Force issued this press release on April 10, 1997, condemning the network:[9]

> The splash around "Ellen's" coming out has turned to waves for one lesbian-owned business because of a decision by the ABC network not to air their advertisement during the upcoming episode when the lead character announces that she is a lesbian.

> The network rejected Olivia Cruise Lines request to buy air time with the explanation that their ad was unfit for younger viewers. Though shooting of the ad has not

Key West Men (Courtesy of Key West).

yet begun, plans called for the commercial to show two women kissing aboard a cruise ship. The company considered the ad to be a compliment to the theme of the April 30 episode. "I'm really disappointed because I was looking forward to being a very proud sponsor of this show," said Judy Dlugacz, founder and president of Olivia Cruise Lines, based in Oakland, California.

Some have called ABC's decision to dock the ad "a double standard" considering that the network is willing to broadcast a show about a lesbian discovering herself. "As more gay and lesbian-themed programming begins to air, network executives will have to take another look at their advertising policies," said Kerry Lobel, Task Force executive director. "They don't seem to have a problem running an ad for other cruise lines with happy straight couples kissing and being romantic," she stated. "Aren't there children watching those programs too?" she asked.

Key West pink (Courtesy of Key West).

Olivia founder Judy Dlugacz told the Commercial Closet, "ABC basically said that 'lesbian lifestyles belong in programming, not advertising.' We were the only ones who wanted to do an ad on that show – everyone else was actually trying to pull their ads – but because we were a lesbian company, they didn't want to air us... on a show that is featuring a lesbian coming out of the closet. We went ahead and made it anyway because we thought we could run it on the local affiliates".[10]

Olivia was forced to purchase local stations, going into five cities: New York, San Francisco, Los Angeles, Miami and – of all places – Winston-Salem, NC. All cities saw the edited version, which removed shots of hand-holding and cuddling between the women. Still, Ellen's coming out show got its highest ratings ever (36.2 million viewers nationally).

In 1998, RSVP Vacations ran a series of 30-second television spots, produced in-house, on the Bravo Network during a

Key West women (Courtesy of Key West)

television program called, The Ellen DeGenres Story. According to Mike Wilke, the ads did not use models but are shots of gay and lesbian guests enjoying RSVP Vacations. This commercial has no voiceover, but includes the graphics "Freedom," "Adventure," "Romance" and "Relaxation." The images are romantic and include a kiss from two men and women holding hands.[11]

It was not until June 2005, that a destination would become the first in the world to air a television commercial geared directly towards the gay traveler. That destination was Philadelphia and the commercial is called, Penn Pals. Created by the Greater Philadelphia Tourism Marketing Corporation and produced by the Altus Group. Thanks to the team at Philadelphia's Comcast Spotlight, especially Jim Gallagher and Ann Letizi, the Penn Pals ran on Comcast-owned cable operators in cities such as New York and Boston on channels including Bravo, Comedy Central, MTV, VH1 and 24-hour gay network LOGO. Through an innovative partnership between GPTMC and Orbitz, the television commercial ran in other major markets as well.[12]

In 2006, Key West aired its television commercial, Freedom, with a middle-aged male couple with an arm around the other appears and the narrator says, "The freedom to be." The commercial aired on LOGO, the 24-hour gay channel from Viacom.[13]

"It sure as hell wasn't easy to produce Penn Pals," said Sharon Rossi. "There were many road blocks and the first was there was no money. The second road block was that something like this was never done before so there was no way we could research what anyone else had done".[14]

> Once Meryl Levitz, our president and CEO, gave us the green light, we decided right then and there that we were not going to cut corners. It took nearly six months to create. We were so lucky to get a top notch creative person. At first, no one knew what the core message would be. But we did know that we wanted to break out from what was obvious. We defined our competitive asset as history. We could have defined it as anything but we knew were not a cruise line or a resort with umbrella drinks. What we did have was history and a place where freedom mattered and we thought if we could cut it right it would resonate. It had to be funny. For Philadelphia, the gay television commercial was the only television spot to go nationally. We were able to air it nationally because the opportunities were so few compared with mainstream networks. I knew the publicity surrounding the commercial would go all over the world and reach more people than paid media could ever do.

Reflecting back on this historic milestone on a train to Philly from New York City on a cold fall day, Rossi said, "there were hundreds of people who made it happen and all of us were very proud to do it. We got so much for so little. More than $100,000 in goods and services were donated to make this commercial."

Moving forward, Rossi offers this advice for the next destination marketer who creates the next gay ad for a destination: Do research first but do it in a different way. Today, there is some history that can be very useful. If she had to do it again, Rossi says she would keep the creative, as she thinks it is very funny, upscale and respectful. If she could change one thing she would probably buy regional markets and do focus groups within those markets first to test the creative before she made the first media buy.

What are the hallmarks of a gay television commercial? It must be sensitive, upscale and funny because people can laugh at themselves and gay men can *really* laugh at themselves.

Choosing the right agency

This is a hard one! This question comes up time and time again, do you need use an agency that specializes in the gay market? Or, does the agency need a gay person working on the account to be successful? The answer is a firm no but it helps. Here is a little secret: A well-known gay tourism slogan was created by guess who, a straight creative director working at a gay-owned agency.

There is a great value in working with gay-owned agencies or an agency that has developed a history of working within the gay market. I have found that when you work with an agency with solid experience in the gay market that you immediately earn credibility with your local stakeholder group because they feel that you will "get it." You also benefit from the vast network of contacts and relationships that have been developed for other clients. Take for example, Witeck-Combs. Bob works with American Airlines, Wal-mart and the Travel Industry of America. Another argument to hire an agency with gay marketing experience is because typically gay marketing budgets are small and need to be highly efficient to make an impact. There is little room to make mistakes. Also, when you launch your gay marketing campaign, it will be watched very closely by your stakeholders, so there too you want to make sure you get it right.

When it comes to media buying, not every mainstream media buyer is well educated on the rapidly changing media marketplace. Can mainstream agencies buy gay media? Absolutely! You don't need a gay-only media buying agency. On one hand, compared to the mainstream market, there is not as much gay media so it can be easier. Here is where it gets complicated. In just the last two years, there has been an extraordinary change in the gay media marketplace. The gay media also tend to be much more advanced in terms of new technology to reach the gay consumer. Gay media were using social media tools and online behavioral targeting before most mainstream companies were. The gay media marketplace is growing and there are more options, but in general, you are talking about reach and frequency. More, whereas in mainstream media, you have to talk to a lot of people with a lot of different demographics and psychographics. In gay media you are still mainly talking to gay men. That is starting to change but it is a slow process. Gay men are much easier to talk to than almost anyone on the planet. You still have got to understand the basics of media buying and know what you are doing to be effective. It is not overly complicated. In fact, most times the sales person is very accustomed to teaching the first-time advertiser or novice media buyer.

Here are some questions that you should ask yourself when considering the right agency:

1. Is the agency familiar with the latest gay tourism marketing research? Be careful of any agency presentation that relies too heavily on "me-search" and does not present an in-depth analysis of the current state of the gay travel market.

2. Do they have a proven track record in the gay tourism market? Is this their first time?

3. Does the agency have a good knowledge of your destination as well as your competitive set destinations?

4. How will their work complement what you are already doing and how will they work with your existing media buying and creative agency?

5. What more does the agency bring to the table? What other companies does this agency do gay marketing with?

6. Does the agency have gay market media buying expertise and do they have personnel on staff that are very familiar with the gay market? This is very important because for so many of us, the gay, lesbian, bisexual and transgender (GLBT) budget is relatively small. Therefore, it is essential to have your limit dollars go a long way. You will be amazed at how many gay media outlets are out there for you to invest your advertising dollars. It is essential that you target our primary feeder markets and buy the media that is best for you.

7. Choose an agency that is skilled at online media buying. All of the research shows that gay and lesbian travelers are more online than any other group. It is essential to have an agency that understands online media buying.

8. Does the company engage in good business practices including having a non-discrimination policy or making domestic partnership benefits available to its employees. Does the company participate with the local GLBT community?

The best practices of public relations

The very first step is to create press materials that are relevant to your destination or travel product. Writing your first press kit for the gay market should include a short release on the history of the GLBT community in your area. It may include significant dates like the first time a gay pride march was held. Or, perhaps, something famous happened in your place that was done by a person in the GLBT community. For example, Tennessee Williams wrote some of his books in Key West, Florida. If you are a hotel chain, cruise line or airline, perhaps this release is a history of your support of the GLBT community or a backgrounder on how and why you began your efforts in the GLBT marketplace. This piece serves to answer the question, why are you gay-friendly?

The next step is to create a calendar of events that might be of interest to the gay community. Keep in mind that the events do not necessarily just have to be gay only, such as a gay pride event. The events can also be of gay interest such as a flower show or an antique show. I find that it is difficult to promote events more than a year out, so I find it best to stick to a yearly calendar of events that is updated twice to add more detail to the calendar of events as the event planners make it available.

Original photography of real gay people enjoying your destination or travel product is essential. Avoid buying stock photography at all costs. While shooting photography is expensive, it is well worth the investment. A picture really is worth a thousand words. Be sure that your photography is diverse; includes both gay men and lesbians, and multiracial couples, if possible. Be sure to have your models or subjects provide a signed release that allows you to use their photos for publicity or advertising. Using pictures from gay events, even if given to you by the event producer, is dangerous. You may not know if the person in the picture signed a release and more importantly, you never want to accidentally "out" someone through your publicity effort, especially if they were just enjoying a day at the gay pride festival. In Philadelphia, I asked two friends of mine to pose for a photograph in front of the Liberty Bell. They are holding hands. That picture was used in USA Today, in national gay magazines, in advertising, on VHI, CNN and *The Daily Show* with Jon Stewart. No one, including my friends, had an idea that this picture would become famous. It is a very good thing everyone signed a photo model release.

It is also important to have a media relations professional who is familiar with the gay market. Your publicity person should be well versed in what is appealing about your destination or product for the gay market. The PR person does not have to be gay, although it helps. It is good practice to develop a network of gay spokespeople who can discuss different aspects of the destination or product to the media. You may consider gay community leaders, chefs who are gay, small business owners (including the bar owners) or people in the arts and culture scene. These people provide depth to a story or press release, make great photo subjects and also provide a well-rounded picture of your destination.

Building a custom media database is critical and should be your first priority. Here is an insider's tip. US Newswire has a gay and lesbian media package that goes nationally and is monitored regularly by regional and national gay media outlets. US Newswire has no annual membership fee and charges per release. It is a highly effective tool to get your message out to the widest gay media audience possible. Another option is to work with agencies like Community Marketing, Andrew Freeman & Company, or FH Out Front, a division of Fleishman-Hillard public relations firm. Each of these firms has cultivated an extensive media database and has earned an exceptional reputation among the gay media.

Press trips are the best way to get the word out. They are low-cost, high-impact vehicles to showcase the best that your destination has to offer to a very wide audience. Gay press trips are slightly different than your mainstream travel journalists. Gay press trips tend to center around a particular event of gay-interest (i.e., a gay festival) and nightlife is usually essential to the story.

Here are 10 tips for gay press trips learned over the years:

1. Never start a press trip earlier than 8:30 in the morning. Usually the press just gets home a few hours before from checking out the bar scene.

2. Gay press trips work best in medium to small groups, six is usually a good number.

3. You can mix gay men and lesbians on the same press trip. I have found that to be the most fun-filled with the most interesting conversations.

4. Be professional. Nightlife and entertainment is a part of the job and gay press trips are fun. As host, just don't have too much fun.

5. They do like to see the destination or partake in the mainstream activities. It does not have to be all-gay, all the time.

6. Always bring local members of the GLBT community to dinners and to functions. The gay media are always looking to discover that local vibe, immediately.

7. Choose a gay-friendly hotel and gay-owned or gay-friendly restaurants and not just your member organizations. Often,

the gay bars or gay restaurants may not be members of the convention and visitors bureau but it is important to show off the gay attributes of the community. In this case, you are doing your destination a disservice.

8. Gay media outlets tend to be smaller with fewer than 20,000 circulations. Even small is big in the gay market. Local gay newspapers and regional magazines may not have the largest readership but they have a loyal readership. The guidelines you typically use for press trips may not be the same here.

9. Racy content. In general, it is best to keep your travel stories out of magazines and newspapers with a high sexual temperature. It can be done. It is harder in Europe, however, I have found that keeping travel stories to glossy magazines, radio and television travel shows and regional newspapers is the best way to avoid any stakeholder issues.

10. Always ask the visiting journalist for recommendations of other good freelance journalists who they work within the gay market. The gay market is filled with freelancers, some good and some bad. There is a network of exceptional freelance travel writers covering the gay market and in general, they tend to know each other.

Here is another insider's tip. Most gay magazines are working on a much shorter long-lead schedule than their mainstream counterparts. You can always find opportunities to promote your destination in the calendar of events section. The editorial content also provides for more ongoing shorter items. For example, *The Advocate* Magazine is published twice monthly.

There is a growing need for b-roll for gay-friendly destinations. In 2006, the Travel Channel aired its first hour-long show on gay-friendly destinations. LOGO, the network owned by Viacom, has regular travel show called *Round Trip Ticket*. In Canada, Pink Planet has an audience of more than one million people and is aired on a mainstream television channel. Those destinations that have b-roll are in the position to take advantage of the exposure that comes with being on television.

Don't ignore the mainstream media in your effort to communicate your message to a larger audience. The mainstream media will reach more gay travelers than all of the gay media outlets combined. An increasing number of travel sections of local newspapers are now regularly covering gay travel. In fact, the Toronto Star now has a regular gay travel column.

Your online press room will be an important tool for you to help communicate your gay tourism tactics. All your gay content and gay-related photography should be posted on your online press room. It is not necessary to separate your gay content from your mainstream content for media.

The gay media landscape

In the past, gay media companies were typically small businesses owned by a few people and mostly had regional reach. For our purposes, I want to focus on the future of GLBT media. For a great read on the history of gays and lesbians in the news media, read Straight News by Edward Alwood (Columbia University Press, 1996). It will give you the history of the rise in the gay media.

Wik Wikholm wrote about the nation's first national gay and lesbian magazine, *The Advocate*, on Planetout.com. Wikholm produces www.gayhistory.com, an introduction to modern gay history.[15]

> The Advocate first appeared in 1967. That first edition was the brainchild of Dick Michaels and his lover Bill Rand, of the Los Angeles activist group PRIDE. In an attempt to improve the group's newsletter, the two created the *Los Angeles Advocate*, a 12-page paper laid out with a typewriter, with 500 copies printed on cheap 8-1/2 × 11-inch stock. In 1969 Michaels and Rand renamed the paper *The Advocate* and began national distribution. By 1974 press runs routinely ran to 40,000 copies.

Today, gay media in the United States consists of hundreds of gay and lesbian newspapers, national and regional magazines, radio, national cable television networks with free and on-demand programming and lots of online Web sites.[16]

The future of gay tourism media campaigns will be integration. You will begin to see the gay media companies create multi-platform media buys that will include online, print, radio, direct-to-consumer and newspaper all in one buy because of the extraordinary change in the gay media landscape. Today, there is a media consolidation trend, where smaller companies are becoming larger companies. This is a huge benefit for gay and lesbian tourism marketers. For the first time, tourism marketers can cast a wider net to reach more gay and lesbian consumers in a simpler way. What remains unknown is how effective these new partnerships will be in driving business to advertisers and if the media will become more expensive now that it is becoming bundled.

The largest gay and lesbian media company is Planet Out Partners, founded in 1994 by Mark Elderkin. Planet Out Partners began simply as a domain name, gay.com. In 2004, it began trading on the Nasdaq under the ticker LGBT. In 2005, Planet Out acquired LPI Media Inc. including *The Advocate*, *Out Traveler*, *OUT*, the largest circulation LGBT magazines in the US, as well as the Web sites Advocate.com, OUT.com and e-commerce sites. Planet Out also owns a number of specialty publications that are not travel related. In 2006, RSVP Vacations joined the Planet Out family. In 2007, the company promises to debut a series of initiatives for the lesbian traveler, which holds great promise for marketers looking to reach these women.[17]

The year 2006 was a turning point for Wilderness Media and Entertainment, founded by LOGO creator and Philadelphia native, Matt Farber. Matt has created a company with interests in LOGO television, Twist radio, Instinct magazine and even a performer, Miss Richfield 1981, a popular Provincetown act. In January 2006, Farber premiered another media first, RADIO WITH A TWIST, the first national gay and lesbian syndicated radio program. The two-hour weekly show premiered with 60 million listeners in 8 of the 12 top US radio markets. Prior to RADIO WITH A TWIST, gay and lesbian programming was produced and aired in individual markets, usually during late-night, weekend time slots. The format included news, information and entertainment by gay and gay-friendly artists. Other content is featured through a partnership with Instinct Magazine. In May 2006, another significant milestone was reached when Instinct Publishing, LOGO founder Matt Farber's Wilderness Media & Entertainment and AOL announced the launch of the RADIO WITH A TWIST, a free 24-hour music, information and lifestyle radio station for the LGBT audience on the AOL Radio Network.[18]

here!, America's first gay television network founded in 2002 by Paul Colichman offers subscription video on-demand entertainment through satellite and all major market cable providers. In May 2006, here! Networks acquired Hyperion Interactive Media (HIM) Corp, an online network of 20 portals and 50 partner Web sites.[19]

LOGO, owned by Viacom, launched on June 30, 2005, as the United States, first advertising-supported national gay television network. Operating on a different business model than here!, LOGO's programming is available for free to more than 20 million households. In 2006, LOGO acquired three Web sites 365gay.com, AfterEllen.com and AfterElton.com. Also in 2006, LOGO became available wirelessly on Amp'd; made programming available for download on iTunes, Amazon Unbox and Google Video; and has added Video on Demand.[20]

Lastly, the National Gay Newspaper Guild represents the best LGBT local newspapers in the nation and has a member circulation larger than the leading national LGBT magazines combined. Member publications include Bay Area Reporter, San Francisco; Bay Windows, Boston; Between the Lines, Detroit; Dallas Voice, Dallas; Frontiers, Los Angeles; Gay & Lesbian Times, San Diego; Houston Voice, Houston; New York Blade, New York; Philadelphia Gay News, Philadelphia: Southern Voice, Atlanta: Washington Blade, Washington, DC: The Weekly News, Miami; and Windy City Times, Chicago.[21]

Cross-promotions work

One of the most effective low-cost tools in gay tourism marketing is promotion. By donating a cabin, airfare or a hotel stay, your product is immediately relevant to that particular group of people or cause. Travel is one of the most sought after items. People always want to be somewhere else than where they are right now. Identify your key feeder markets and an event where you can stand out. It was the best way to raise your profile in more cities than you could afford to purchase advertise in. It is a good way to generate word of mouth buzz. It also provides a way for non-profit organizations to raise money. Some organizations used trip giveaways as a silent auction item to raise money. Most times, the trip raises more money for the organization than you could have ever given in a monetary donation.

Promotions can also include cross-promotions between other destinations and gay-friendly vacations. In theory, gay travelers should want to travel to other gay-friendly destinations. Therefore, one of the best places to influence where a gay traveler may go next is by marketing to them while they are on another vacation. Most major gay tour operators, especially those who charter cruise ships, are always looking for sponsors. Major gay events, including the Gay Games, are also now partnering with other destinations to promote travel.

Philadelphia took the concept of cross-destination gay marketing to new heights by signing deals with RSVP Vacations, R Family Vacations and Club Skirts, an event during the Dinah Shore Golf Classic in Palm Springs all in one year. At the same time, Philadelphia also created cross-promotions at gay film festivals in Toronto, Montreal, Washington, DC and Connecticut. Philadelphia also gave trip giveaways at the Human Rights Campaign annual dinner and the annual GLAAD Awards. One of Philadelphia's most successful promotions was the $100,000 Ultimate Gay Stay Giveaway. We were able to purchase $50,000 in advertising and get a matching bonus of an additional media of $50,000. There were two trip giveaways, one for lesbians and one for gay men. We tied the trip giveaway to an annual event, Equality Forum, to help raise this event's national profile. The promotion included Internet, radio, television, magazine, newspaper and even exposure on board an RSVP cruise ship. The results were amazing. This one promotion doubled GPTMC's gay travel database.

Direct to consumer expos

Gay Life Expo in New York City is the largest direct to gay consumer expo in the United States, produced by HX Media. As much about image building as it is about sales and marketing, the expo is traditionally held in November and organizers claim more than 20,000 GLBT consumers come through the convention center during the two-day event.

Gay consumer expos and their gay travel expo counterparts are among the most important tools in creating word-of-mouth about your travel product. There has been an enormous growth market among travel companies looking to market directly to gay consumers.

What is the benefit? First, you have the opportunity to come face to face with the gay consumer. In an age where the travel industry is increasingly losing face time with their guest (primarily through the ease of Internet purchase and check-in kiosks), it is important not to lose sight as to whom you are marketing too. Second, the gay consumer expos allow you to answer questions directly from self-identified gay travelers. Interestingly enough, I have overheard the most basic questions being asked, like what is there to do in Philadelphia. Or, how do I book your cruise? Consider gay expos as part sales tool, part brand building and part focus group.

Travel expos that caterer exclusively to the gay traveler is another huge growth segment. Community Marketing, Inc. invented the gay travel expo concept and has produced more than 100 Gay & Lesbian World Travel Expos in the United States and Canada since 1993. Every year, the expos have steadily grown in attendance among both the travel trade and consumers drawing nearly 100,000 people since they first began. The Gay & Lesbian World Travel Expos became the preferred place where gay-friendly destinations, travel and hospitality companies came to do business.

In June 2006, Community Marketing announced the sale of its Expo division to HX Media LLC. HX Media produces the Gay Life Expo in New York every November and publishes HX Magazine and the New York Blade newspaper. Since taking over, they have re-branded the Gay & Lesbian World Travel Expo to the "Gay Life Travel Expo." With a dedicated team onboard, HX promises to expand the Gay Life Travel Expos to more cities across North America in 2007 and beyond, and will add amenities such as destination workshops and multi-media presentations. There are a series of gay travel expos that you can find easily on the Internet.[22]

Tips for exhibiting at a gay travel expo:

1. Identify your primary feeder markets and if budgets are tight, exhibit in just those cities. Use cross-promotions to open up other markets.

2. Distribute collateral materials that speak directly to the gay and lesbian travel market.

3. Create an attention getting device to draw people to your table. Some destinations, like Dallas, have brought attractive cowboys with their shirts off. Do bring your local drag queens or mascots to get attention.

4. K.I.S.S. Keep it simple stupid. Don't overcomplicate your booth. It only increases your cost to produce, ship and distribute.

5. Be very interested in where your booth is positioned and try to be grouped into a travel pavilion if possible.

6. Leverage your media buy to get a free booth space at a major expo. Many of the major national gay and lesbian magazines are sponsors of the gay expo series. Ask your advertising representative if they will throw in a table as part of your advertising budget.

What issues resonate with the GLBT community?

Simply put, anything that is relevant to the GLBT community will resonate with your audience. Gay marriage, gays in the military, gay and lesbian civil rights, health issues including HIV/AIDS, breast cancer, domestic partnership benefits, anti-discrimination policies and politics. Now, the trick is, what do you avoid and what do you align your organization with? The answer is pretty much dependent on your business and your destination. The fact is, you have to choose one that is a right fit for your product, your employees and your corporate giving guidelines.

For example, some marketers align their products with the Human Rights Campaign (HRC) because of its highly brand-loyal, affluent and easy to reach membership. On the other hand, some marketers may shy away from HRC because of its political advocacy work. Meanwhile, Kimpton Hotels has for more than 20 years assisted HIV service organizations across North America through employee volunteerism, HIV educational campaigns, corporate donations and raising funds through special events as part of its Red Ribbon campaign. American Airlines sponsors a wide range of events of interest to the GLBT community.

Collateral materials

Typically, destinations first start with a simple brochure or map of their destination. It is a low-cost, consumer friendly way to communicate what your destination or product has to offer. This is essential. Gay travel collateral materials have come in many forms from simple two-panel brochures to multi-page detailed travel planners.

Can you just use your general market brochure? The answer is no because unless your general market brochure shows same-sex couples or utilizes "gay" code, it will not be meaningful to the gay consumer. I think of the 2006 Princess Cruise Line brochure that I received from Princess. Even though I would be sailing their ship in February 2007 as part of an RSVP all-gay charter, the company's brochure does not have one image, one logo or anything that signals that it may be a good cruise line for a gay traveler. There is nothing relevant to me about the Princess brochure except the ship. Also ask yourself, is your mainstream copy written in a funny, engaging way that uses vocabulary that communicates with the intended reader? Most general market brochures do not include the names and addresses of local gay bars or gay event calendars. Investing in a gay travel planner or brochure is the first authentic indication that you are specifically asking a member of the GLBT community to visit. It is important to update your brochure regularly. Annually is best; however, every two years is still acceptable.

For destinations on a tight budget, consider a partnership or a sponsorship of an existing travel guide or map. Columbia Fun Maps Publisher, Alan H. Beck, is the most experienced person in the gay map publishing business.[23] His maps can be found in nearly every gay bar and coffee shop in the United States and Canada. The company is making plans for expansion to Australia and Africa. Beck creates brilliant, low-cost, but highly effective partnerships with tourism offices. In most major cities, the tourism agency works with his publication to develop content, imagery and distribution channels. FunMaps reaches users across the US and Canada and gives them update information on how to plan a trip from their home destination to anywhere that FunMaps promotes. Columbia FunMaps launched a brand new Web site in December 2006 to coincide with the publication's 25th anniversary. The dynamic Web site allows travelers to post information, make reservations, buy tickets and other items and list from up to 150 from cities around the world. Soon, the FunMaps Web site will have interactive maps that will connect tourists with businesses in the gay districts. Through the T.A.G. approved hotels, more than 750 hotels are listed online and in the maps. Increasingly, tourism agencies in cities where there are FunMaps utilize the FunMaps to support their marketing programs including Toronto, Vancouver, NYC & Co, Miami, Seattle and others.

Another low-cost but effective option to consider is sponsoring or promoting a Gay.com TravelGuides, powered by the travel brand OUT & ABOUT. These destination guides are specific to destinations or travel themes such as romantic vacations, sex and travel or the women's guide. They are offered to consumers at no cost at gay.com.

Gay brochures do not have to be very expensive or large. They can be a well-designed two-side piece on glossy paper if that is all you can afford. Most importantly, the information must be current, inviting and specific to a gay audience.

Be strategic about your distribution. Make sure your brochure is available online for download on your Web site and the Web sites of your gay-owned and operated accommodations. Don't forget to include your visitor center, local gay community center (if you have one) and gay coffee shops and bars. These are the locations that gay travelers will be looking for information. Also, most destinations distribute collateral at gay expos and gay pride festivals to generate interest in visiting. Philadelphia has found good success at leveraging our media buys where we have been able to distribute our trip planner at major events including Gay Days in Orlando. It is a good rule of thumb to print about 30,000 pieces to get you through a full year of marketing activities.

Online marketing: the key to closing the sales

There are literally millions of Web sites with gay content out there. Online marketing offers travel companies the best opportunity to reach the wired and traveling GLBT consumer. All the research shows that gay and lesbian travelers are more likely to shop for and buy travel online than their heterosexual counterparts. Best of all, online media is much more measurable than other forms of media. You know if your online is working or if it is not. According to a number of travel industry and advertising sales representative sources, online spending is growing at an extraordinary pace. In the past, just 10 percent of the marketing budget was dedicated to online. Now, some destinations are now dedicating 50 percent and more of their budgets to online marketing.[24]

Online marketing is smart marketing. It is essential to making the sale. Remember, according to the Community Marketing study, at least 81 percent of US respondents purchased travel components on the Internet in the last 12 months. About 81 percent of all US respondents purchased airline tickets online, 80 percent purchased accommodations online, 65 percent rented a car using the Internet and 76 percent of those who took a cruise in the last 12 months indicated that they purchased at least one cruise online.[25]

Justin Garrett, director of media sales for travel, is one of the industry's foremost experts on online tourism marketing campaigns geared towards gay travel. Justin has more than 10 years of online experience working at the two largest online companies that sell travel, Travelocity and Planet Out.[26]

"Let me start by saying that I am not at all surprised at the research that gay and lesbian travelers are buying most of their travel online because they are a highly wired market segment," said Justin in a phone interview from his San Francisco home. "The rise in gay travel really does go back to 9/11 when the general market stopped traveling and people were afraid to leave their hometowns but gay people were still traveling. I think growing up gay you have to be brave naturally and that translates to the world around you."

According to Justin, gay people are spending on average 1.25 hours online with Planet Out compared to 30 minutes for the general marketing and that includes sites like Yahoo where people are checking mail. He sees a new trend in online advertising now where advertisers are planning their online buy for the gay market first, then they go on to plan the traditional media to support the online buy. That is a significant shift from how online travel media was planned and bought just a few years ago.

Here are a few of Justin's tips to build an effective online advertising campaign.

First identify your online goals. Are you selling rooms or cabins or are you building a brand? To build brand, you want to make sure you have brand interaction and highest reach within a media network. What are those areas online where you can do that? Sometimes it could be in social networking or chat rooms. When selling a hotel room or a destination, a marketer may choose to purchase a regional buy from those key feeder markets close to their area where they can have higher visibility. It is very important to have a balanced media mix recognizing that online has a tremendous reach. Another competitive advantage of online marketing compared to national media outlets is that buys can be directed regionally through geo-targeting and even behavior targeting.

Second, turn to the creative. All online advertising campaigns must have all the hallmarks of any good creative. For the gay market, it is really important to show gay people in the creative. Justin calls it humanizing the gay creative.

Gays and lesbians like to see themselves in the advertising. It is easy to do and it should always be tasteful. Two people of the same sex can be depicted simply as having a conversation or two people standing side by side enjoying the view. You can share a life experience in a non-sexual environment.

When advertisers ask me how can they improve their results? I say add people to the creative. Click through rates is higher for humanizing the creative compared to a standard market message.

A few more of Justin's tips are as follows:

- Utilize general market online knowledge but with a gay twist.

- Use strong creative with your logo in each frame.

- Frequently update your creative to stay fresh during the online campaign, if your budget allows.

- Your message must be clear and concise.

- Use animated creative, use flash and try three loops of animation.

- The last frame must be your take away message.

- Always build to an offer.

- Evaluate your campaign every month.

Finally, as with any new market, Justin recommends staying the course because it takes a long time to build brand loyalty online. He also warns of tokenism marketing. Avoid being a first-time advertiser who wants to test the gay and lesbian segment.

"Some companies will see an article in *Newsweek* or *Advertising Age* and read about the income and see the online numbers and want to drop in an online advertising campaign and expect to automatically make a killing," continued Garrett. "The gay and lesbian consumer are ultra savvy and they know when they are being targeted for their dollars."

Orbitz is a leading online travel company offering consumers the widest selection of low airfares, as well as deals on lodging, car rentals, cruises and vacation packages. In summer 2002,

Orbitz became the first leading online travel agency to offer permanent content and deals for the gay and lesbian travel community, with the launch of their "micro-site" featuring information about gay-destination cities and events on six continents, specially tailored travel deals and tips for gay parents traveling with their families.

Senior Director E Marketing Jillian Balis for Orbitz is responsible for online marketing at travel giant Orbitz, a company that itself pioneered gay tourism marketing online. Any marketing effort that drives traffic to Orbitz.com is under her domain. Marketing to the gay and lesbian traveler is a big initiative for Orbitz.[27]

Balis says that the goal of any online gay travel marketing campaign has to drive traffic directly to your Web site and preferably directly the landing page with content of gay interest. Marketers should focus on paid search building campaigns and target those other Web sites that gay and lesbians frequent. Of course, the major search engines are very important, especially the natural rankings. It is essential to understand the words that gays and lesbians use when booking travel to maximize your search engine optimization. Finally, it is very important to constantly test and refine your online creative to see what resonates with the gay traveler. Some companies have changed their online creative several times during the same campaign.

The first challenge is to get consumers to your Web site, but the job does not end there. The idea is to engage consumers with your site through content and then to convince them to buy travel products.

"You must land on a web page that is consistent with the marketing and offers consumers gay travel content, imagery and travel products," said Balis. "You must have content that speaks specifically to gay and lesbian travelers. The content should feature destination information, gay-friendly businesses and imagery with gay men and lesbian women. The key is to covert the online looker into a sale. If you don't make the sale, you can earn more revenue to re-invest in marketing."

She says that having rich gay content prominently on your Web site gives you the competitive advantage of keeping gay travelers on your site longer thus giving you an opportunity to sell travel products and more importantly to improve sale. For some online travel Web sites, you can make some money on the airfare but the real profit comes in by selling hotels and cruises. Because gay travelers have different interests, it is important to have a wide range of activities on your site from outdoor to nightlife to arts and culture.

Remember, it doesn't necessarily have to be all-gay, all the time. A run along Kelly Drive in Fairmont Park in Philadelphia for example is of interest to gay and to straight people. (However, it may very well be the best place to catch guys with their shirts off during the day. That is of gay interest!)

Gay content plays an important role in fostering a sense of comfort and familiarity with your site among gay travelers, whether it is for business or for leisure. Gay travelers are not looking for anything different than other travelers, really. They may be gay but they are also looking for value, affordability, and they do want to be able to identify gay-friendly hotels, airlines and destinations easily so they can feel safe and welcome in their travels.

"The gay and lesbian travel market is an important part of our corporate philosophy and strategy," said Balis. "Gay and lesbian travelers do travel frequently and they are loyal Orbitz customers. We are the first online travel Web site to focus on the gay and lesbian travel segment and it has been a very good and profitable experience for Orbitz. We always get emails from people who object to our gay marketing effort, however, it pales in comparison to those who support it."

How does Orbitz measure its success? Two words: sales and profitability. For Orbitz, the gay customer has been a good customer for the online company. They spend more compared to certain other segments and they return to Orbitz to book travel again. Orbitz also engages in a brand tracking study and has tracked it over time. Gay and lesbian travelers have an affinity for the Orbitz brand.

In November 2005, American Airlines became the first US Airline to launch a vacation package Web site for GLBT travelers, www.AAVacations.com/rainbow. The goal is to attract millions of loyal GLBT customers. AAVacations offers tour packages that combine air travel, hotel and rental car. The AAVacations.com/rainbow Web site boasts more than gay-welcoming destinations.[28]

Mark Elderkin, President and Founder, Gay.com, said that the bigger challenge that lies ahead in advertising to the gay market is to make the offer relevant and authentic, especially for non-travel products like beverages and cars.[29] He suggests the following four advertising tips:

1. Target your audience

2. Target message with the product

3. Extend your general market campaigns to gay market

4. Choose right media mix. (e.g., lesbians are more "word of mouth" and viral compared to gay men.)

To summarize this chapter, here are the 10 marketing mistakes you should avoid:

1. Do not use straight people in gay advertising creative. Gay people will spot a wolf in sheep's clothing. Don't buy stock photography. It has been seen over and over again.

2. Embrace your brand. You don't necessarily need an entirely separate marketing campaign for the gay traveler. They want to know what you are offering and that they are specifically invited.

3. Show real gay and lesbian people not just fantasy imagery. Avoid the cliché of showing shirtless men with beautiful bodies, even if you are selling a cruise or beach vacation. Show real looking lesbians not the fantasy lesbians that some advertisers are tempted to use.

4. Don't promise what you can not deliver. For example, are you really the new, hot gay destination? Or, is your gay pride event really the best in the world? Don't offer a gay welcome kit with your hotel package if the hoteliers are not prepared to fulfill it.

5. Don't repurpose creative intended for the straight audience in gay media. It just will not work.

6. Don't bury information for gay and lesbian travelers. Place it prominently on your Web site or in brochures. Gay travelers should not have to work harder than everyone else to find the information that they are looking for.

7. Don't be boring! Advertising can be humorous without being offensive.

8. Don't quit too soon. It takes time to build an image as a gay-friendly destination or travel supplier. You may not see immediate results or sales over night. You must stick to a marketing program over time. I recommend a three-year commitment.

9. Don't put all your eggs in one basket! Be sure to have a diversified media mix to achieve your desired results. As gay media becomes more expensive, be sure to allocate enough dollars to this market to keep pace.

10. You do not you have to be gay to be successful in this market and don't assume that your marketing message will only influence gay people. People who are parents, friends, relatives and co-workers with GLBT people will also positively respond to your message.

Case study

Stereotypes in advertising

Mike Wilke, founding executive director, The Commercial Closet [30]

Commercial Closet Association is an organization that educates and influences the world of advertising to understand, respect and include lesbian, gay, bisexual and transgender (LGBT) references in advertising to achieve a more accepting society while achieving successful business results.

The Commercial Closet collection contains more than 2,000 global advertisements from 33 countries, including over 700 gay marketing print ads. How important is Mike's work, instrumentally important. You don't think that there is homophobia in advertising? Consider these ads in the Commercial Closet Web site:

- Five men are crowded into a truck, and four uncomfortably pull away from one of the men because he's singing a woman's song (a commercial for Chevrolet Colorado, 2005).

- A cable TV installer is slapped on the rear by a football player, then dashes for the front door (a commercial for DirectTV, 2001).

- A taxi drops a man off in the wrong place, a threatening transsexual approaches (Adidas, 1999).

- A high school student has girls fishing through his pockets for a prize, he cowers when a guy approaches (Sprite, 2000).

- A young man accidentally lands in the arms of an old man while waiting for his girlfriend, the old man smiles (Zima, 2001).

According to Mike Wilke, more than $427 billion worldwide in advertising (and $175 billion in the US alone, per ZenithOptimedia) is spent annually to convince people to buy things – many of those ads contain messages about GLBT people and how others should treat us.

You never, ever want to perpetuate a stereotype or worse yet, make the GLBT community the butt of your humor. Commercial Closet Association recommends asking these critical questions before the creative is approved.

1. What is the intent for including a same-sex come-on reference, GLBT storyline or person in the first place?

2. Is the gay community the subject of a funny punch line or stunt?

3. Are audiences intended to laugh at a same-sex "threat," the GLBT person, and/or sympathize with the negative response from a straight person?

Be sensitive to GLBT stereotypes; avoid demeaning references to gay/lesbian sexual practice, and derogatory language. Advertising often stereotypes, but beware of complications. Portraying a feminine gay man is an old idea that alienates people. Straight-male-fantasy "lipstick lesbians," duplicitous bisexuals, and deceitful/scary transgender people are narrow clichés that are polarizing.

Here are some commercials that violate this principal:

- A spokesman in a prison professes not to bend over but then gets locked in with a too-friendly prisoner (7Up, 2002).

- Four guys go camping and flee when they hear the banjo song from "Deliverance" (Saturn, 2002–2003).

- A man hiding under a bar gets reamed by a bartender mistaking his rear for a bottle opener (Bud Light, 2002).

- A guy in an upside-down clown suit wants to eat a hotdog, through the clown's rear (Bud Light, 2003).

Be inclusive and diverse. Whenever people are shown, integrate GLBT individuals/family members/friends/couples, reflecting varied ages, races, genders, etc. Language references to family, relationships or gender should not be hetero-centric.

A few best examples are as given below:

- Class reunion mentions people who "came out" (John Hancock, 2001). Men and women want M&M girl (Mars, 1999).

- Three couples (gay, lesbian, straight) fight and make up (MTV, 2000).

- Gay youth talks about being disliked (Levi, 1998).

- Gay couples as business partners (American Express, 1999. IBM, 1998).

Avoid insults to masculinity or femininity. GLBT people are frequently attacked in life for not meeting gender expectations. Consider these two commercials:

- A man uses the word "cute" and is told to get in touch with his "masculine side – fast!" (T-Mobile, 2003).

- "She's a he" is written across the chest of an attractive male-to-female transsexual (Sauza Tequila, 1997).

Do good research. When conducting general research or forming new mainstream campaigns, GLBT perspectives should be considered and included as often as possible. Don't limit their input only to gay-targeted messages.

Be consistent and confident. Modifying or withdrawing ads suggests waffling and creates further trouble. Respond to criticism with business rationales, like diversity and the bottom line. Avoid time-restricted airings of commercials unless they legitimately deal with sexual situations inappropriate to youth.

For an advertising timeline, visit www.thecommericalcloset. org.

Expert soapbox

The Daily Show with Jon Stewart

Gay = Cool

Meryl Levitz, president and CEO,
Greater Philadelphia Tourism Marketing Corporation [31]

Just after Philly's gay television commercial first aired in 2005, *The Daily Show* with Jon Stewart called the Greater Philadelphia Tourism Marketing Corporation. Reporter and Comedian Rob Corddry wanted to investigate for himself what was so gay about Philadelphia?

What followed was a hilarious four-minute segment that featured Mr William Devlin, vice president of the Urban Family Council, a conservative group often opposed to homosexual issues, Ben Franklin and me. Ben was there to show Rob "a gay ol time in Philadelphia."

What did the segment on *The Daily Show* with Jon Stewart really mean for Philadelphia? *The Daily Show* with Jon Stewart made a big difference in who noticed our gay tourism campaign and who noticed Philadelphia. Let me start out by saying that the producers of the show were very nice to me. To be honest, I was nervous when I was watching the show. They have total editorial liberty but they decided that I was the "straight man" to Rob Corddroy and Rob was the straight man to Bill Devlin. We were not the joke tellers, Rob was. It was a classic comedy sketch where everyone played their roles.

Let's go back to the big picture. Getting Philadelphia into popular culture was an overarching goal in general and to have Philadelphia on a show as hip as Jon Stewart's was a huge win. Keep in mind, Philly's gay tourism campaign had already been featured on the Hollywood Squares and VHI, but this was

Jon Stewart. His show was a number one hit on Comedy Central. His show drew a very young, affluent, hip audience.

Here is how I can explain it best, usually when Philadelphia is featured on CNN and MSNBC, I get calls from friends of mine. When Philadelphia was featured on *the Daily Show* with Jon Stewart I got calls from my friends children. They would say, "Oh Mrs. Levitz, I saw you on the Jon Stewart show that is so cool." They would go on to say that the best thing that every happed to Philadelphia was being on Jon Stewart. Then, I would get emails from the kid's parents who told them that Philadelphia was on the Jon Stewart show and that the parents were proud of Philly too. In one national television segment we were able to put a hipper image on the Philadelphia brand for a whole new audience while still reaching our core market, the parents.

Right after the segment aired, the Philadelphia Inquirer picked up the story immediately. I remember getting a call from the editorial page editor, Chris Satullo who asked why didn't you tell me that I was going to be on the Jon Stewart show? The next day, he ran an editorial congratulating GPTMC for taking one for the team. The win with the editorial was that the reach of the Jon Stewart show was immediately extended. Because this very positive article ran on the Editorial page in the Philadelphia Inquirer, the gay campaign was immediately blessed. So it was ok.

And, it didn't end there. The segment was also available on the Web from *the Daily Show* with Jon Stewart Web site and the reach was huge and extended even further. GPTMC was told that this particular video clip became the most forwarded video on Yahoo that day with hundreds of thousands of people saying, you got to see this segment. Then the conservative talk shows picked it up including, Bill O'Reilly, and that perpetuated the story. We were cool and we were cool online too.

Perhaps the greatest lesson for tourism marketers in this 24/7 media and online age is that a story can gain momentum very quickly and it is important to make sure your stakeholders are well informed of what you are doing and why.

Case study

Ft. Lauderdale, Florida
An overnight success, 10 years in the making!

Richard Gray[32]

Richard had opened up The Royal Palms Guest House in 1991, the first B&B's in the area to cater exclusively to GLBT guests.

At that time, people were coming to Ft. Lauderdale for about one night and then would continue on to Key West, Florida to spend about seven nights in the Southernmost Point, just 90 miles from Cuba.

Ft. Lauderdale didn't have a gay "buzz" at the time and when Richard would ask travelers at trade shows about their perception about his city it usually evoked negative connotations to the Spring Break crowd. During the early 1990s, gay and lesbian travelers were more interested in South Beach, a Florida resort whose renaissance was well on its way. Like most small business owners, Richard said he couldn't afford to launch a huge marketing campaign, so he needed to find another way.

Back then, Ft. Lauderdale's gay business community wasn't really organized but it did have a Gay Business Association. The association was mostly made up of local bar owners who were preoccupied with local affairs and competition amongst themselves. They really never had an interest in tourism marketing. So, Richard did his own advertising for quite a while but was really limited in what he could do.

By 1993, Richard was elected to the Executive Board of the International Gay and Lesbian Travel Association (IGLTA). It was here that he met his mentor, Walt Marlowe. Walt was a brilliant teacher and mentor for Richard. He had owned Alexander's Guest House in Key West and he invented the gay cooperative advertising model. Essentially, Walt convinced his fellow Key West B&Bs to market themselves together in one page of advertising with one unified look in an effort to share the costs among a number of advertisers and to brand the destination. Walt would later move to Ft. Lauderdale and began to oversee the office of the IGLTA. He has since passed away.

In Richard's role at IGLTA, he used the opportunity to speak on panels to start to sell Ft. Lauderdale as a gay-friendly destination. As vice president of IGLTA, he convinced the Ft. Lauderdale CVB to host its first media familiarization trip with gay media. Nikki, Francine and the team at the Ft. Lauderdale CVB believed in the power of gay tourism to help them in the overall goal of changing the destination's image and brand. Nikki Grossman shares credit with Ed Salvato and the media on those first familiarization trips as one of the best and most important strategic decisions that led to building Ft. Lauderdale's image as a gay-friendly getaway and a new gay hotspot.

As time went on and the destination matured, more accommodations opened that catered exclusively to the gay market. Ft. Lauderdale grew from one B&B to seven in just a few short years. 1996 was a turning point year for Ft. Lauderdale because now there was a critical mass of business owners whose livelihoods depended on tourism. More importantly, all of the properties contributed to the bed tax which gave them a voice within the tourism community. It probably helped that Richard had earned a credible reputation in the gay market because of what he had achieved through IGLTA. With so much favoring gay tourism, Richard thought the time was right to approach the Ft. Lauderdale Convention & Visitor Bureau. He met with CVB president Nikki Grossman and the Vice President of Communications Francine Mason and asked them to dedicate advertising dollars to the gay and lesbian market.

They were all for it but here was the deal: the CVB would allocate $25,000 to advertising in gay publications if the owners of the gay accommodations would match it. Richard approached the other accommodations and said let's work together to promote the destination. He went door to door explaining to his fellow B&B owners that everyone would save money and they would be sending the right message to the consumers that Ft. Lauderdale as a strong gay product offering. Richard reasoned that the consumers will make their decision on where they spend the night only after they made the decision to come to Ft. Lauderdale in the first place. Thankfully, his fellow B&B owners agreed and he was able to take advantage of the CVB deal. Nikki and Francine had the foresight and the courage to recognize that gay travel was important to invest in. They first started with baby steps and fairly quickly became gay aggressive.

Taking what he had learned from Walt, Richard put together Ft. Lauderdale's first gay cooperative advertising program, modeled after the one in Key West. The CVB did the creative for the ad and we officially came out in a full-page ad in the Advocate Magazine in 1998 with the *Immerse Yourself* ad featuring that they call, Bubble Boy.

Richard's relationship blossomed with The Fort Lauderdale CVB and he was invited to become their gay market liaison. He joined Ft. Lauderdale CVB marketing advisory committee in 2002. Together they branded the destination. The CVB relationship grew slowly but steadily. They have built a bridge between the gay community and the tourism promotion agency. Today, even the big hotels recognize that the gay market is a crucial component to their economic well being. Ft. Lauderdale is spending a little more than $400,000 in gay and lesbian marketing to include print and online advertising, press trips and International trade shows. Each year, the Ft. Lauderdale CVB includes an entire section on the gay market at their annual meeting at the convention center to the Broward County hospitality community.

"As our liaison to the local gay community since 1996, Richard Gray has been instrumental in Greater Fort Lauderdale's

Immerse yourself Bubble boy (1998–2000) (Courtesy of Greater Fort Lauderdale Convention & Visitors Bureau).

gay tourism success," said Francine Mason, vice president of communications for the Greater Fort Lauderdale Convention and Visitors Bureau. "Not only are we proud to have The Royal Palms, owned by Richard Gray and voted PlanetOut editor's choice as best gay resort, in our backyard, but we are so fortunate to be able to tap into Richard's global tourism marketing contacts."

Ft. Lauderdale became the first CVB to add a gay icon to their Web site, sunny.org. Today, a full 20 percent of the visits to sunny.org click through the Rainbow section of Sunny.org and the site is consistently one of my top referrals of business. It is very helpful that The CVB gives each accommodations owner a free listing on the site.

The gay business community is still growing in Ft. Lauderdale and with growth comes growing pains. The accommodation sector is the most cohesive and the most successful. Richard and others created the Rainbow Alliance, a non-profit organization dedicated to the mission of increasing GLBT tourism. Every innkeeper is a part of it. There are 50 members who meet monthly. They created a guide map that they distribute at the accommodations and at trade shows. The Rainbow Alliance buys advertising in addition to the CVBs advertising buy to extend the reach. Richard sees this group as a potential foundation for a Gay Chamber of Commerce. However, there are some challenges still ahead. As in most cities, the gay bar owners and gay-friendly restaurants do not work together to bring in more tourists. Perhaps the gay-owned bars and restaurants would see more business if they advertised in cooperative tourism ads because increasingly gays and lesbians are staying in mainstream hotels rather than all-gay accommodations. The mainstream hotels rarely offer the local gay newspaper on the premises and their hotel concierge may not be educated on the gay market. At some point, Richard predicts the organization will need a full-time paid executive director to take our organization to the next level.

"His non-stop dedication to Greater Fort Lauderdale and the gay hospitality partners keeps us competitive as more and more destinations vie for the gay traveler," said Mason.

Notes

1. Gay Press Report, 2005, Prime Access and Rivendell Media.
2. Rossi, Sharon, Vice President, Advertising, Greater Philadelphia Tourism Marketing Corporation, in-person interview, October 25, 2006.
3. Wilke, Mike, Founder and Executive Director, The Commercial Closet, www.commercialcloset.org, October 2006.
4. Holden, LoAnn, writer, in-person interview, Miami, Florida, September 9, 2006.
5. Roth, Thomas, President and Founder, Community Marketing, Inc., in-person interview, September 2005.

6. Clarke, Jayne, in new television commercial, Orbitz Has Gay Travelers In Its Sights, USA Today, August 1, 2003.

7. Orbitz, Orbitz to Debut Its First-Ever Gay Travel Commercial During Gay Pride Month, press release, June 9, 2003.

8. Wilke, Mike, Founder and Executive Director, The Commercial Closet, www.commercialcloset.org, October 2006.

9. National Gay and Lesbian Task Force, Ellen Misses the Boat, press release, April 10, 1997.

10. Wilke, Mike, Founder and Executive Director, The Commercial Closet, www.commercialcloset.org, October 2006.

11. Wilke, Mike, Founder and Executive Director, The Commercial Closet, www.commercialcloset.org, October 2006.

12. Greater Philadelphia Tourism Marketing Corporation, Ground-Breaking TV Ad Set To Promote Gay-Friendly Philadelphia, June 2, 2005.

13. Wilke, Mike, Founder and Executive Director, The Commercial Closet, www.commercialcloset.org, October 2006.

14. Rossi, Sharon, Vice President, Advertising, Greater Philadelphia Tourism Marketing Corporation, in-person interview, October 25, 2006.

15. Wik Wikholm, www.planetout.com/news/history/archive/advocate.html, November 1, 2006.

16. Hopkins, Jim, Media Offers New Outlets for Gay Audiences, USA Today, March 2, 2006.

17. Planet Out, Incorporated, www.planetout.com, November 2006.

18. Wilderness Media & Entertainment, www.wildernessmedia.com, November 2006.

19. here! networks, here! networks acquires Hyperion Interactive Media Network of Gay On-Line Sites and Print Magazine, press release, May 10, 2006.

20. LOGO, www.logoonline.com, November 2006.

21. National Gay Newspaper Guild, www.nationalgaynewspaperguild.com, November 2006.

22. Community Marketing, Inc., Community Marketing, Inc. Announces Sale of its Gay & Lesbian World Travel Expo division to HX Media, LLC, press release, June 20, 2006.

23. Beck, Alan, Columbia Fun Maps, interview, November 1, 2006.

24. Garrett, Justin, Planet Out Inc., phone interview, November 2006.

25. Gay and Lesbian Tourism Profile 2006, Community Marketing Inc, San Francisco, CA.

26. Garrett, Justin, Planet Out Inc., phone interview, November 2006.

27. Balis, Jillian, Senior Director, E Marketing, Orbitz, phone interview, November 10, 2006.

28. Carrancho, Young, American Airlines, phone interview, November 3, 2006.

29. Elderkin, Mark, International Gay and Lesbian Travel Association Convention, speech, Washington, DC, May 27, 2006.
30. Wilke, Mike, Founder and Executive Director, The Commercial Closet, www.commercialcloset.org, October 2006.
31. Levitz, Meryl, Greater Philadelphia Tourism Marketing Corporation, interview, September 5, 2006.
32. Gray, Richard, The Royal Palms, phone interview, September 23, 2006.

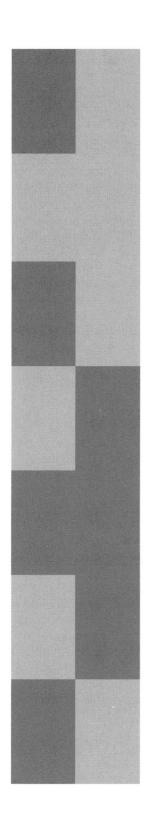

How do you know if you are gay-friendly?

Greetings from Asbury Park! Sitting on the balcony of my newly renovated hotel room at the beautiful Empress Hotel, I realized the economic power of gay tourism. It is a Saturday night in August 2006 and the hotel is sold out. The pool is surrounded by dozens of tourists who have come to Asbury Park, New Jersey, a town that remains virtually abandoned especially compared to its very wealthy neighboring towns.

Asbury is an atypical beach resort. Founded in 1870, the legendary Asbury Park, home to the Stone Pony and once the vacation spot of U.S. presidents, is now experiencing an incredible renaissance fueled by gay tourism. Since the 1970s the town has been virtually abandoned. Ironically, Asbury Park is sandwiched between the wealthiest beach towns in New Jersey, yet looks as though a hurricane destroyed most of the buildings. Miles of ocean front property is vacant.

The Empress Hotel opened as a luxury resort for vacationing families in the 1950s. In the 1970s, when Asbury Park began its decline, the hotel began to decline as well. After struggling for years, the hotel closed in 1988, opened in 1991 and closed again. In 1998, music producer Shep Pettibone bought the abandoned building and opened Paradise Nightclub inside. The nightclub lured crowds of gay travelers away to the beaches of Asbury Park. Some floors of the hotel reopened in August of 2004 and the full renovation will be completed in 2007.[1]

What makes Asbury Park gay-friendly? For now, simply, one hotel, one nightclub, two bars and a small gay beach, but these simple things are fueling the resurgence of a legendary town.

So this leads us to the million dollar question: How do you know if your travel product is gay-friendly? Ed Salvato, from Planet Out, says half-jokingly, while sipping a cocktail with an umbrella in it at the Loews in Miami Beach, "It is like when Supreme Court Justice Potter Stewart said, 'how do you know something is obscene, you know it when you see it' and the same is true for what is gay-friendly, you know it when you see it."[2]

Ed's point really is that being gay-friendly is not solely scientific. There is no checklist set in stone but there are steps you can take to be sure you are gay-friendly. It is an experience and an environment that someone just feels. You can just feel it when someone is "friendly," "welcoming," "tolerant," "bigoted" or "indifferent."

Gay-friendliness will vary from destination to hotel to transportation company. It is more like there are indicators of gay-friendliness in travel. However, there are few obvious indicators.

Ultimately, you and your GLBT guests will be the best judge of your own product. However, you may have difficultly identifying what is gay-friendly and what is not.

First define your product. Is it gay, gay-friendly or gay unfriendly? For destinations, gay-friendly is easier to define. Do you have gay events? Do you have an active gay community and/or gay bars and restaurants?

How can a travel product be gay-friendly? Take travel insurance. How can travel insurance be gay friendly? Well, Travel Guard International provides trip cancellation, medical emergencies and baggage "Coverage for you and your domestic partner."[3]

What about a car rental company? Enterprise Rent-A-Car and Avis both waive their additional driver fees for non-married couples if you are gay or lesbian.[4,5] Some companies still charge gay and lesbian couples an extra fee simply because they are not technically "married" under the law. This is a very gay-unfriendly policy.

There is no such thing as a gay airline. Yet, American Airlines has without question distinguished itself as a gay-friendly airline. What does the airline do to communicate that it is gay friendly? First, it created the Rainbow TeAAm today led by openly gay employees George Carrancho and Betty Young. The airline was the first to implement same-sex partnership benefits. It also has progressive non-discrimination policies extending protection for both sexual orientation and gender identity (transgender). Since 1991, American Airlines earned 100 percent on the Human Rights Campaign Corporate Equality Index. For nearly a decade, American Airlines has been a sponsor of gay and lesbian events throughout the United States, including the Gay Games in Chicago.[6]

Gay travelers love this airline, and at a time when airlines are competing to fill every seat on price and for customer loyalty, this gives American Airlines a strong competitive advantage over its competitors. Interestingly, in 2006, Southwest Airlines, a conservative Texas company, launched an advertising campaign aimed at increasing that airline's share of the gay travel dollar. Delta Airlines, Air Canada and Icelandair are also actively courting the gay traveler.[7]

For hotels, there are a number of simple ways to know if the property is gay-friendly. Does the hotel concierge know where the local gay bars are? Is your front-desk staff trained well enough that they are anticipating that gay travelers will be checking in and they avoid silly stupid mistakes, such as asking two men if they really want just one king bed? Hotels that are gay friendly demonstrate it both discretely and "out" loud. A discrete hotel may advertise in gay and lesbian publications, host gay press trips and train the staff. A discrete hotel may also belong to the IGLTA and use just its logo on its website or in gay advertising. Some hotels sponsor local gay events, which often is marketed online. Sponsoring local gay events not only shows your gay-friendliness but it also generates lots of business.

For some gay travelers, another telltale sign that a hotel is really gay friendly, and not just providing lip service, is if that hotel is willing to sell a gay customer the same type of entertainment that hotel sells a straight customer in the privacy of their own hotel room. If a hotel offers in-room adult entertainment geared toward the straight traveler then it should sell adult movies of interest to the gay community. If by selling a gay traveler adult entertainment, pornography, in the privacy of his or her own room when the gay traveler is willing to pay for it, the hotel can make a profit, why would you not offer that? Isn't selling adult movies to gay people the best way to determine if your hotel has gay travelers, at least sometimes?

In 1998, Community Marketing created the Travel Alternatives Group, commonly known as TAG. TAG's mission is to identify companies and organizations that welcome gay and lesbian hotel

109

and B&B guests, and then help them get the word out, increasing sales and generating repeat business through word of mouth. It is a program for small boutique hotels to internationally flagged chains.[8]

For a very affordable $150, accommodations get a slew of good benefits including a partnership with Travelocity that allows TAG properties the exclusive right to be listed on Travelocity's gay travel microsite. In addition, TAG-approved hotels are listed in a directory that goes to 45,000 gay consumers, 3000 travel agents and 2000 meeting planners. For more information, visit www.tagapproved.com.

To qualify as an accommodation that is TAG Approved®

- Enforce non-discriminatory policies including "sexual orientation."

- Treat heterosexual and domestic partners equally in personnel policies.

- Provide diversity and sensitivity training for employees.

- Employ staff that reflects the diversity of the community, including gay and lesbian employees in all levels of employment.

- Empower customers and employees to be "watchdogs" of your gay and lesbian business practices.

For destinations, either you are gay-friendly or you are not gay-friendly. It is that simple. You can not invent gay-friendliness. It is not created, it simply is. What it really comes down to is *what* about your destination might be considered gay-friendly? Most places, both large and small, have a gay pride celebration. Other destinations have a gay film festival or annual gay event that celebrates the diversity of the community. Of course, it is usually important to have a gay bar or dance club for nighttime entertainment. Make an inventory of what your destination has to offer. It is a misnomer to think that your gay event or gay nightlife has to be the "very best" to be of interest to gay travelers. In fact, two major U.S. cities, New York City and Miami, have seen a major transformation in their legendary gay nightlife scene. In 2006, the world famous Roxy Nightclub, where Madonna made her appearances when promoting her new albums, closed its doors to the dismay of gay club-goers everywhere. Miami has seen its gay nightlife scene facing strong competition from Ft. Lauderdale during the 2000s. Typically, what is most essential is that the GLBT community has an opportunity to meet other people like themselves in relative safety.

Word of mouth is usually more powerful for a destination than most marketing. Key West, Provincetown and Palm Springs are very well known gay destinations. Up-and-coming gay-friendly destinations include Las Vegas, Phoenix and the west coast of Florida. It is interesting that local politics does play a role within your destination's reputation as gay friendly. Vermont with Civil Unions and Massachusetts with gay marriage laws play a huge role in making a destination gay friendly. Typically, but not always, how the local community embraces the GLBT community makes the strongest case for a destination being perceived as gay friendly.

All destinations are not the same

Believe it or not, there is a wide spectrum in gay-friendly travel in the world today depending on what continent you are on at the time. Ed Salvato says that Europe doesn't dwell on matters of sexuality like we in America do.[9]

> People don't bat an eyelash anymore when two guys or two gals check in. Europeans have moved beyond the sex part of homosexuality to the legal aspects of homosexuality. In the cities there is an acceptance and tolerance that it is just a part of everyday life.

He continues, "As for Canada, that country has been always gay friendly. Now that gays and lesbians have legal relationship status with similar rights to marriage, the gay market is always part of the marketing plan and has become a part of normal business practices. Gay people are 100 percent equal."

In the United States, oftentimes it often depended on whether you were a red state or a blue state. Red is synonymous with the conservative party, the Republicans, and Blue with the progressive states, or the Democrats. People in the United States are still preoccupied with the sex part of homosexuality. Gay travel remains a political hot button and a weapon for conservative and religious groups who believe that gay = sin.

Typically, major urban centers tend to be more naturally gay-friendly than their rural counterparts. However, it is incorrect to believe that gay-friendly destinations are limited to big cities. Take for example, Bloomington, Indiana. Bloomington is a totally accepting environment but is located far from the big east-coast and west-coast cities. (See their amazing case study later in this chapter.) New Hope, Pennsylvania, is another shining example of gay-friendly getaways that were, well, born gay.

Key West is the best example of a small town that was born gay![10] Home to Tennessee Williams and U.S. president Truman, Key West attracts more than 650,000 gay and lesbian visitors each year. Looking at Key West's independent spirit dating back to its original founding and even through the Civil War, it should come as no surprise. Key West was the first city in Florida to officially recognize same-sex marriage (although it is not recognized by the State of Florida or any other Floridian county). Today, about a dozen bed and breakfasts cater to the GLBT traveler and offer the distinctly Key West experience, especially the famous sunsets. Key West is a city that is undergoing a huge transformation due to the impact of the cruise ship industry. Now, a popular U.S. port, every day thousands of straight passengers disembark and invade the tiny island. Some argue that Key West is less gay-friendly because of the cruise ship industry. Yet, the town survives because of the work of the Key West Business Guild and Key West's annual events.

Are there gay-hostile destinations? Sadly, yes. Unfortunately, there are areas of the world that are simply known for not being safe for gays and lesbians. In some countries, like India, gay people can be imprisoned for life.[11] In 2006, Amnesty International updated its "Sexual Minorities and the Law: A World Survey." The report can be found at www.ai-lgbt.org and is worth reading to see how your destination treats GLBT people under the law.

> In many parts of the world, being gay or lesbian is not seen as a right, but as a wrong. Homosexuality is considered a sin or an illness, a social or ideological deviation, or a betrayal of one's culture. Whereas most governments either deny practicing human rights violations or portray them as rare aberrations, the repression that GLBT people face is often openly and passionately defended in the name of culture, religion, morality or public health, and facilitated by specific legal provisions. In some countries, AIDS has been labeled a "gay plague", and homosexuality "the white man's disease". Same-sex relations are dubbed "unChristian", "unAfrican", "unIslamic" or a "bourgeois decadence". Some governments seek not only to exclude lesbian and gay people from local culture, but also to deny that they are members of the human race. (Amnesty International, Act 40/016/2001).

A number of incidents including hate crimes and religious protests have occurred in the Caribbean islands, which has earned this area of the world a reputation as unwelcoming to the gay and lesbian traveler. From the late 1990s through even the mid-2000s, all-gay cruise ship charters have found limited ports of call in the Caribbean whose people and business welcome gay tourists, and one horrific hate crime against four gay tourists vacationing in St. Maartten made international news. One very notable exception is the uber gay-friendly Caribbean hot spot, Curacao. Why is this?

> Although laws proscribing homosexual relations are defended in the name of local cultural values, such laws in many Caribbean countries are a legacy of the colonial past. The passionate defense of "sodomy" laws by certain Caribbean governments perpetuates discrimination and creates a climate conducive to violence against lesbian and gay people, both at the hands of state officials and of others in the community. In a submission to the UN Human Rights Committee on Trinidad and Tobago in October 2000, AI stated that the retention of laws which treat homosexuals as criminals lends support to a climate of prejudice which increases the risk of attacks and other abuses against people believed to be gay or lesbian. Reports suggest that such laws are often used by the police to extort money from members of the gay community. (Amnesty International, Act 40/016/2001).

Expert soapbox

Are you gay-friendly? Ask yourself these questions

Ed Salvato[12]
Global Travel Editor, Planet Out Inc.

1. To be gay-friendly, you must come up with the reason why you would want to cater to the GLBT market. You may love the gay and lesbian market for the money but do they love you back? Why are you in the gay travel business in the first place?

2. Do you share values and the concerns of the gay and lesbian traveler? Are you even aware of the current issues that are important to the community as a whole?

3. Do you know who your customers really are? Are they gay men or lesbians or both? Be careful how you answer this, can

your product be all things to all gay people? Sometimes yes, sometimes no.

4. What exactly is the product you are offering? Why might it be of interest to gay and lesbian travelers? Is your hotel clothing optional, which may attract some gay men travelers while alienating lesbian travelers?

5. Do you penalize gay couples with extra fees because they are not technically a 'married' couple under the law? For example, do they have to pay an extra driver fee when renting a car while their straight married counterparts do not have to pay this fee?

6. Are you a destination that hosts a gay event at a particular time of year? For example Aqua Girl or the White Party in Miami. Do you sponsor local GLBT events all year long?

7. Have you trained your employees? Behind the scenes, how do you treat your own GLBT employees? Do you practice what you preach, even if it costs you money?

8. Have you dedicated enough money to marketing to the gay and lesbian traveler and are you willing to stay the course with a long-term commitment?

Perhaps this is a good time to discuss how gay events become destination definers and how it shapes the image of your destination as gay-friendly. The GLBT community is certainly not a one size fits all group. Therefore, there is an event that appeals to nearly every kind of gay traveler.

Provincetown, Massachusetts, is a prime example of the many kinds of people living in the gay community and what kinds of events draw them to a particular destination. Here is a sampling of annual events that are held in Provincetown.[13]

- Eighth Annual Circuit Week held around July 4th weekend

- Provincetown Summer Bear Week also held in July

- Carnival Week held in August

- Wine Lovers Weekend held in March

- Holly Folly, 9th Annual Gay and Lesbian Holiday Festival

- Meet Your Man In Provincetown Held in November

- Twenty-second Annual Women's Week

- Mates Leather Weekend, held late September

- Women's International Flag Football Association

- Eleventh Annual Family Week

- Single's week

Another great example of perfect gay-friendly event is, Key West's Fantasy Fest, which brings 10 days of masquerade balls, outrageous costume contests, and uninhibited behavior. The week ends in the Captain Morgan Fantasy Fest Parade. In September, Key West hosts WomenFest, bringing 5000 lesbians to the island in Florida's historically "off-season." Perhaps, the most magical time of year in Key West is New Year's Eve when Drag Queen Sushi is lowered to Duvall Street in a red high heel shoe. Take that Manhattan!

Sometimes events put your destination on the gay map. Take for instance South Beach, Miami, Florida. Here annual events are tied to key tourism seasons. The White Party, the Winter Party and Aqua Girl draw tens of thousands of gay tourists who love to dance on the beach in their city each year.

In Philadelphia, Equality Forum, an international, educational and film organization holds its annual event each year in May. Where else but in Philadelphia, the birthplace of liberty and freedom, should an annual event spotlighting contemporary GLBT issues and struggle for equality be held?

Can a cruise line be gay-friendly? Absolutely! First, cruise lines can ensure that their cruise director offers "Friends of Dorothy" meetings on each of their cruise itineraries. Friends of Dorothy meetings, or FODs, are a veiled reference to Dorothy from the 1939 classic film *The Wizard of Oz*.[14] Since most gays and lesbians understand this term, they know that is where they can discreetly meet other gay and lesbian passengers. According to the Cruise Critic, the most open and accessible cruise lines that offer regular FOD meetings are the larger lines such as Norwegian, Carnival and Princess.

Still, there is more that cruise lines can do and they should do more. Cruise lines should empower gay and lesbian employees to host FOD meetings on board each sailing. In addition to the Friends of Dorothy meetings, mainstream cruise lines can work with travel agents who can connect the cruise line with local GLBT organizations to bring their gay group on board ship. Each year, Philadelphia's Chumley Singer, one half of the famous Carlotta and Chumley, sells around 200 cabins to a GLBT affinity group that he organizes each year. Cruise lines also have the option to focus their gay and lesbian marketing on select mainstream cruise sailings and advertise that "mixed" cruise in gay and lesbian media to help fill cabins. Also, having out gay staff in visible positions on board ship also signals that this cruise line is gay-friendly. Finally, educate everyone from travel agents, to on-board staff and operation staff.

"Most gay cruises are sold by straight women," says Kenneth Kiesnoski, Destinations Editor for *Travel Weekly*. "90 percent of the gay cruise product is sold by straight women. Operators need to educate travel agents. Don't forget the straight middle man or middle woman to sell your cruise as gay-friendly."[15]

> In many ways, gays and lesbians are no different than the straight consumer when selling cruises. What the agent or cruise line is selling is gay-friendliness. Cruisers are interested in the wow factor, bragging rights and value.
>
> Gays are the dream cruise customer. They spend more on incidentals and special restaurants reservations. They sail more often and spend more. It is not a matter of social policy, there is money to be made in gay.

Today, there is fierce competition among cruise lines for gay vacation tour operators, like RSVP Vacations, Atlantis and R Family Vacations, to charter one of their ships. The gay tour operator heavily advertises their ship to the gay and lesbian traveler and also provides, in many cases, an opportunity for a gay passenger to try their cruise line first before any other.

Case study

Bloomington, Indiana
The "gay" but not "all-gay" destination in the Midwest United States

Rob DeCleene[16]

> The verdict: Whether you're gay, straight, or somewhere in between, Bloomington offers something rarely found in this country: a small town with a bold history of openness and acceptance.

The Bloomington Convention and Visitors Bureau (CVB) has nine full-time and six part-time staff with a budget just shy of $1,000,000. A little more than 30 percent of the budget is dedicated to tourism and the gay market is included in that area. Between 2000 and 2006, the CVB spent around $35,000. In other words, the gay market made a huge return on a relatively small investment. The only funding stream for the CVB is a bed tax.

Where did it all begin? In 2000, a chance meeting between bloomington CVB executive director Valerie Peña and Tom Roth, president of Community Marketing, Inc., captivated Peña's attention. Valerie met Tom at an International Association of Convention and Visitors Bureaus' (now known as Destination Marketing Association International) CEO Forum, where Tom was speaking to the group about the future of GLBT travel. Tom was planning the very first Gay & Lesbian Tourism Conference in New York City and Valerie attended. She is a straight woman from Oklahoma City. Bloomington, Indiana, and Indiana University both extend domestic partner benefits to significant others and now, gender identity and sexual orientation are covered in the city's human rights ordinance. While, the CVB played no role in any of those successful initiative offering gay benefits, these do play a role in the marketing of the destination.

Back in 2000, gay tourism was still in its early stages in the tourism industry. Peña was a visionary leader who recognized the economic potential of the market, well ahead of most destinations around the world. No other destination in the Midwest was even thinking about gay travelers, let alone pursuing the market. She studied the demographics of the gay traveler and understood that their discretionary income gave them the power to travel frequently. However, she realized there was still much more to learn about this market and that like every other market segment it would take years to develop.

Gay tourism was really a perfect fit for Bloomington, a liberal and very unique community in the Midwest. Although Bloomington, Indiana, is located in a "red," meaning a politically and socially conservative state, the CVB considers Bloomington a bright blue island in a sea of red. The community is the quintessential college town with a long history of cultural and political progressiveness. The resident population is youthful, bohemian, educated, and, most importantly, extremely accepting of the GLBT community. Bloomington is home to Indiana's first and only radio show dedicated to lesbians and gay men called *BloomingOut*. In 2001, the Human Rights Campaign published a study on the results of the 2000 census which for the first time asked the question, do you live in a same-sex household. Surprisingly, Bloomington, Indiana has the fifth highest per capita population of same-sex couples in the U.S., trailing only San Francisco, Santa Fe, Portland (Maine) and Miami. Both Bloomington and Indiana University offer health benefits to domestic partners, regardless of gender.

Soon after meeting Tom Roth, Peña attended the first International Conference on Gay & Lesbian Tourism. In 2001, Peña hired me. I was immediately given the responsibility of developing the CVB's gay tourism efforts.

My first step was to attend the Community Marketing Gay & Lesbian Tourism Conference to learn for myself about the market and to network and establish contacts in the gay tourism industry. We also used the conference to begin publicizing the CVB's efforts toward this market. The group of tourism professionals attending the conference was, and continues to be, extraordinarily supportive. It was here that I first met Jeff Guaracino from Philadelphia. Bloomington certainly stood out at the conference because it was unheard of at the time for a destination in the Midwest, particularly from a community the size of Bloomington (a population of less than 100,000), to be promoting itself as gay-friendly. Through the knowledge gained at the conferences and the encouragement provided by industry professionals, my colleagues and I were more motivated than ever to expand efforts and really get the ball rolling. Later in 2001 and early 2002, I wrote a marketing plan, which has served as a useful "map" to coordinate Bloomington's efforts.

The next step was identifying GLBT leaders within the community in order to gain their support and inform them of the CVB's intentions toward the gay market. We formed the Bloomington Rainbow Business Guild. Our membership was around 30 people. We established committees and worked to create a solid foundation for the group.

While forming the Bloomington Rainbow Business Guild was a successful tactic, the CVB did spend a year trying to define the mission of the organization. Several members of the group were more interested in establishing a gay chamber of commerce. During our early stages, it became apparent that not everyone shared the same vision as the CVB – to bring people to town and have them spend the night in our hotels. The group began to flourish when we successfully narrowed the group's focus to just tourism and bringing visitors to town. With a shared vision, things quickly began to happen as issues were simplified.

The next step in the process was taking inventory of just what could be marketed to the gay traveler. The CVB quickly established a policy, which is used to this day: "Treat this market as we would any other market segment." In other words, the CVB made a strategic marketing decision to not just market the "gay" aspects of the destination. Instead we would market all the wonderful aspects of our community, whether it was gay or not it would just have appeal to gay travelers as much as it does for straight travelers. We added the gay market into our other markets, and similar to our other marketing programs Bloomington itself is the main attraction. Our goal was to become the top 'gay-friendly' but not 'all-gay' destination in the Midwest.

If you haven't been to Bloomington, our community has many attributes that not only lead to tremendous quality of life for residents but also make a wonderful sell to tourists. It is our destination's natural appeal that would be the focus of our gay marketing effort.

Here is a list of what we promote to the gay market. It may surprise you.

- Three wineries and two vineyards

- The state's largest lake (one of three in the city)

- Internationally renowned performing arts through the Indiana University Jacobs School of Music, including the longest, continuously running opera season in the Western Hemisphere

- The Kinsey Institute for Research in Sex, Gender and Reproduction

- Collegiate and community theatre

- Museums, including one of the country's best collegiate art museums

- Hoosier National Forest, two state parks, and two state recreation areas

- Impressive selection of dining choices that are extremely affordable when compared to larger cities

- Extensive selection of amateur sports as a result of the Division 1-A Big Ten member

- Indiana University Athletics

- Thriving art gallery and antiquing scene

Finally the big day! In late 2002, we officially "came out" as a gay-friendly destination by issuing a simple press release, just one year after the Human Rights Campaign study from the census. The next day, *The Bloomington Herald-Times* ran a front-page story and included our newly designed rainbow-colored logo. The television news stations quickly picked up the story. Our initial marketing strategy was to focus on hosting travel writers to gain free publicity in gay magazines, newspapers and online to gain attention.

Our strategy of focusing on the economic importance of gay tourism and promoting the real Bloomington to gay tourists worked and allowed the CVB to smoothly "come out" to the local and regional media with little public dismay. Of course there was the occasional letter to the editor in the local newspaper objecting to the gay campaign. The general objection expressed concerned that local tax dollars were being used for gay tourism. This was ironic, given the fact that the CVB is funded completely by a bed tax, levied only on people spending the night in a hotel room in the county. And, of course, the CVB only used bed tax dollars spent by gay tourists!

The next step in the process was to focus on event development. We wanted to attract more gay audiences and we needed an annual gay event to help with our publicity efforts. First, the CVB became actively involved in the "Sexual Minority Youth in the Heartland Conference" held on the Indiana University campus in 2002 and again in 2004. The conference attracted several hundred youth-serving professionals from across the country for sessions about working with sexual minority youth and how best to assist them through the early stages of their journey.

After the conference, we turned our attention to gay film and assisted two graduate students from Indiana University in creating the PRIDE Film Festival. From their initial idea and vision, a committee was formed and the first festival took place in January 2004. It was a one-day event. Today, the PRIDE Film Festival is completely community planned and includes screenings on campus in the student residence halls. PRIDE now attracts an attendance of over 1500 people and is a four-night festival. This annual event is important in our ongoing marketing efforts.

By the end of 2004, another critical step in Bloomington's evolving gay tourism campaign occurred. The movie *Kinsey* was released in theaters nationwide. The film was based on famed researcher Dr. Alfred C. Kinsey and Bloomington is home to the Kinsey Institute. Bloomington hosted one of three national premieres, with the others in New York and Los Angeles. The resulting publicity, combined with favorable reviews of the movie, resumed the ongoing discussion of the importance of Alfred Kinsey's study to the gay rights movement, and, indeed, in many ways identified Bloomington as an integral part of these groundbreaking studies of sexual behavior in the human male and female. Soon after the movie was released, *Out Traveler* magazine sent a travel writer to visit Bloomington. The *Out Traveler* is the most widely circulated gay travel magazine in the United States.

To keep the momentum going, in 2005, we launched our new website, www.visitgaybloomington.com and published

Bloomington's first gay-specific brochure. In the first year, the website became the most popular link from our primary website, www.visitbloomington.com. Nearly 3000 gay market brochures have been sent to individuals from across the United States and even many foreign countries.

Publicity surrounding the efforts of the CVB continued to swirl. Articles about Bloomington's efforts were published in *USA Today*, *The New York Times*, *San Francisco Chronicle*, *Travel Weekly*, gay publications such as *New York Blade* and *Southern Voice* (Atlanta), and, perhaps most famously, featured on Weekend Update with Tina Fey on *Saturday Night Live*. Thankfully Tina Fey chose not to make fun of the efforts, but rather announced them and continued on to mock New Jersey and its hypothetical gay tourism slogans. Bloomington was also featured in a rave review in the *Out Traveler* magazine. Our hard work paid off when we received the prestigious Editor's Choice Award for tourism marketing from Ed Salvato at PlanetOut/Gay.com in 2005.

Bloomington remains committed to gay tourism marketing. Sadly, the Bloomington Rainbow Business Guild is no longer active, although every once in a while, there is discussion of bringing the group back together. We are proud of the success already achieved and extremely motivated to expand our efforts for many years to come. Visit our website, which is continuously updated with new events and activities. In 2007, we launch our first advertising campaign targeting the Midwest. Also, look for the second edition of the gay brochure; a new regional advertising campaign; and more travel stories, and we are bidding on various gay meetings and conventions for 2009 and beyond. So perhaps soon, we'll see you in Bloomington!

Case study

Kimpton Hotels & Restaurants[17]

Founded by Bill Kimpton in 1981, San Francisco-based Kimpton Hotels & Restaurants is the first and leading collection of boutique hotels coupled with chef-driven, destination restaurants throughout the United States and Canada. The hotel group is known for highly personalized guest services and takes pride in its social responsibility programs.

In addition to being an innovative hospitality-industry leader, Kimpton has also been a leader in GLBT equality for well over a decade. This support comes from its progressive roots of forming

Kimpton Hotels (Courtesy of Kimpton).

in San Francisco during the beginning of the AIDS epidemic. In the early years of HIV, Kimpton lost many employees to the disease and was one of the first hotel companies to fully embrace HIV education and care. This overall corporate compassion helped lead the company to embrace other programs too, from environmental causes to helping economically underprivileged women enter the workforce.

With support from top management, Kimpton launched an eight-point GLBT community involvement program in 2002 – setting a new standard for other hotel companies. This comprehensive market strategy earned Kimpton tremendous loyalty in the GLBT community. Kimpton has been recognized with

achievements such as being included as one of the best companies for gay and lesbian employees by numerous GLBT magazines. And in 2002, Kimpton became the first hospitality company
to receive a 100 percent score on the Human Rights Campaign
Foundation's Corporate Equality Index.

Kimpton Hotels and Restaurants GLBT Community Outreach
Program

1. Progressive personnel policies: Using the Human Rights Campaign Foundation's Corporate Equality Index as a guide,
   Kimpton strives to meet all progressive employment practices recommended by the organization. Kimpton has received
   a 100 percent HRC score every year since 2002. In addition, Kimpton provides extensive employee diversity training so that everyone feels comfortable in the Kimpton
   environment.

2. KGLEN: A company cannot be truly gay-friendly without the
   input from its employees. Kimpton formed the Kimpton Gay
   and Lesbian Employee Network (KGLEN) to advise the company on personnel and community outreach concerns. The
   committee meets quarterly and has representation from every
   region of the country.

3. Community support: Kimpton and its employees are comm-
   unity-involved. The company sponsors national and local
   community groups supporting the health, recreational and
   equality needs of the GLBT community. Parents and Friends of
   Lesbian and Gays, Human Rights Campaign, National AIDS
   Fund, National Lesbian and Gay Journalist Association and
   the National and Gay Chamber of Commerce are among the
   dozens of organizations that receive support. In addition,
   every year Kimpton sponsors a Red Ribbon Campaign that
   benefits HIV service agencies on a local level. The campaign
   includes promotional collateral and special events to educate
   guests about AIDS/HIV.

4. Travel program marketing: Kimpton advertises to the gay and
   lesbian community every day. Company advertisements and
   promotions are placed in regional and national magazines in
   addition to gay-specific travel websites.

5. Travel packages: Kimpton offers a wide variety of travel packages for guests, including Pride Packages and gender-neutral
   Romance Packages that are inclusive of everyone.

6. Business to business: Kimpton and business travel have
   always been closely associated. Kimpton is involved with gay

and lesbian business associations throughout North America. Kimpton is especially known for its loyalty among woman business travelers, lesbian or straight.

7. Publicity: Gay and lesbian travelers have been an important part of the success of the company, and Kimpton appreciates their support. Through press and community outreach, Kimpton wants the world to know that the company is gay-friendly. This has resulted in terrific coverage from mainstream newspapers like *USA Today* and the *New York Times* to extensive coverage in gay travel magazines like the *OutTraveler* and local GLBT newspapers.

8. InTouch loyalty program – The goal of the GLBT program is to develop a base of loyal GLBT customers that love Kimpton so much, they will become advocates for the company and individual hotels. The company encourages customers to join the GLBT list of the company's customer loyalty program, InTouch. By the end of 2006, over 10,000 customers will have joined the list and will receive quarterly newsletters about Kimpton's GLBT outreach programs.

Kimpton has created a true culture of diversity within the corporation. A company can have the programs and the action steps, but if it does not have a supportive culture that lets employees be themselves, a diversity program cannot work. The Kimpton eight-point GLBT initiative brought this support to all levels of the company, and has made Kimpton the most gay-friendly hotel group in North America.

Notes

1. City of Asbury Park, New Jersey, www.cityofasburypark.com/history, August 2006.
2. Salvato, Ed, Planet Out Inc., in-person interview, South Beach, Miami, September 9, 2006.
3. Von Metzke, Ross, International Travel Insurance Company Now Covers Domestic Partners, gaywired.com, 2005.
4. Enterprise Rent-A-Car, Philadelphia-Area Enterprise Rent-A-Car Offices Change Rental Policy To Benefit Same Sex Couples, press release, September 9, 2006.
5. Avis Rent-A-Car, www.avis.com/prouder, December 2006.
6. Carrancho, Young, American Airlines, phone interview, November 3, 2006.
7. *Passport* magazine, October 2006.
8. Community Marketing Inc., www.tagapproved.com, November 2006.

9. Salvato, Ed, Planet Out Inc., in-person interview, South Beach, Miami, September 9, 2006.

10. The Florida Keys, History of Key West, www.thefloridakeys.com, October 2006.

11. Amnesty International, Sexual Minorities and the Law: A World Survey, 2006, www.ailgbt.org, November 2006.

12. Salvato, Ed, Planet Out Inc., in-person interview, South Beach, Miami, September 9, 2006.

13. Provincetown Business Guild, Provincetown Gay and Lesbian Guide, www.p-town.org, October 2006.

14. Cruise Critic, Friends of Dorothy Meetings, May 5, 2005, www.cruisecritic.com/cruisestyles.

15. Kiesnoski, Kenneth, Destinations Editor, *The Travel Weekly*, in-person interview, September 9, 2006.

16. DeClene, Robert, Bloomington, Indiana CVB, interview, June 2006.

17. Courtesy of Kimpton Hotels & Restaurants. December 1, 2006.

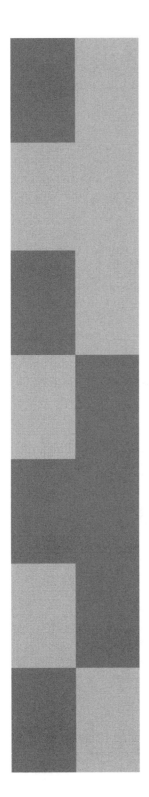

International, group, meeting and convention and corporate

The gay and lesbian travel market is too often considered simply a leisure market segment. Nothing could be further from the truth! Gay and lesbian travel is also international, group, meeting and convention and corporate.

Would you be surprised to learn that 20 gay-oriented meetings have been held in Dallas, Texas, in just 24 months since that city launched its gay tourism marketing efforts in 2004? Phillip Jones, president and CEO of the Dallas CVB, told the *Star-Telegram* that six more events are scheduled for 2007, including a gay rodeo.[1]

There are conventions for gay doctors, gay lawyers, gay journalists, gay civil rights leaders, gay financial planners, gay square dancing associations, gay scientists and technical professionals and annual meetings for gay employee groups representing *Fortune* 500 companies including Microsoft and Disney. There are more than 80 gay and lesbian associations that can be booked as a group meeting or convention. More, this business is often booked out for just a year or two and is perfect for generating short-term business.

Of course, there are also conventions that have nothing to do with being gay, lesbian, bisexual or transgender. It may be a convention or meeting for real estate agents or endocrinologists. However, the opportunity may exist to influence the decision to come to your destination in the first place and the chance to increase attendance at the convention because your city has reputation as a gay-friendly place to visit.

The gay meeting and convention market today

"The GLBT convention market is still in its embryonic stage and is developing towards infancy," said Jack P. Ferguson, senior vice president of the Philadelphia CVB. "The GLBT convention market is considered very niche at present compared to traditional sources of business: corporate, association, trade show and SMERF."[2]

Ferguson said that there are two significant challenges facing sales organizations: the lack of education on how to identify and market to the GLBT meeting planner and the lack of permanent contacts and offices. It is hard for mainstream CVBs and global sales organizations to go after the business because GLBT convention planners are mainly volunteer-driven and hard to reach.

This is the fundamental problem. The hospitality industry is hard pressed to find the names, address and meeting schedules of GLBT groups. GLBT meeting organizers, most of whom are volunteers, may not yet have the knowledge or skill set (and vice-versa) on how to work effectively with sales teams of CVBs and hotels. Another challenge to booking gay meetings and conventions is that oftentimes the planners are volunteers. Volunteers change too frequently or have already decided on where and when they are going to send their business. However, the internet is helping to narrow the search for those organizing meetings and conventions for the gay and lesbian market.

Some tourism professionals predict that the GLBT market will eventually find a home within the social, military, educational, religious, fraternal (SMERF) market. As more global companies organize GLBT employee groups, more corporate sales jobs will include the GLBT market.

Until that time, a brand-new resource is the Gay & Lesbian Convention and Visitors Bureau (www.glvcb.org). The GLCVB is the very first step in solving the problem of the lack of readily identified GLBT meeting planner contacts. Invented by Community Marketing, the GLCVB is positioned to help bridge the gap between the gay community and CVBs. This is a significant step in helping the gay and lesbian meeting develop. The GLCVB will serve as an educational organization helping both sides of the industry.[3]

Working with the GLCVB offers a gay market insight and communications tools to define the approach to the gay and lesbian market, especially for meeting planners, tour operators and travel agents. The GLCVB works with sales organizations to establish goals based on the latest research and market forces. The GLCVB has a strong stable of assets that includes email newsletters, a gay and lesbian tourism directory and an unrivaled database.

Expert soapbox

Ten steps to booking GLBT convention business

Veronica Torres, Diversity Convention Sales Manager[4]
Dallas Convention & Visitors Bureau

Veronica Torres, diversity convention sales manager of the Dallas Convention & Visitors Bureau, is perhaps the most successful CVB sales woman in the country booking GLBT meetings and conventions. Each year, she is responsible for booking more than 8000 hotel room nights attributable to the GLBT market. She has proven that a straight woman can reign. She has set the bar. She has proven that through hard work, a dedication to learn about the market and a fabulous personality anyone can book GLBT conventions and meetings. Here are her tips of the trade:

1. Construct a plan. Write out specific goals that you would like to accomplish and set a timeframe. Develop a model that fits your organizational structure and your overall goals. Write a mission statement to keep you focused. Your plan should answer questions such as, do you want to be a top GLBT convention city? Or, how many room nights do I want to book from the GLBT market? If your budget supports it, start first with GLBT research to help identify your potential market share. Do not construct a plan without first speaking to your local gay chamber of commerce, if you have one in your city, or members of the local gay business community and hotels that share your vision. Whatever your plan is, stay focused.

2. Identify your top 25 accounts (some are listed in the appendix of this book). Research if your city has already been a host for a GLBT convention. For the past 30 years, national GLBT associations have been meeting mostly without the help of a CVB or hotel sales staff. If they have already been to your city, invite them back. Identify the conferences that you would like to host based on what your destination can offer. There are educational conferences, sporting events, health conferences, military conferences and general GLBT meetings and conventions. My advice is to use the Internet to help you narrow down the list. Oftentimes, you will find out lots of information just from the Web, including the time of year of the annual conference, average room rate and organizational information. Assuming you have already partnered with your local GLBT community, consider developing relationships with the leadership in the national GLBT community.

3. Research your city. Take a very close look at what your city has to offer, both gay and of gay interest. Find your own uniqueness that sets you apart from your competitive cities. You will soon discover what will draw conventions and tourism to your destination. Consider all the important factors to any convention planner, such as weather, accessibility through a major airport and hotel availability. What are the gay attributes of your destination? Do you have an annual gay pride festival? Do you have a "gayborhood" with gay-friendly shops, restaurants and nightclubs? Is that neighborhood close to a hotel or the convention center? Signature events in your city will help draw more people. Create a gay calendar of events. Try to use what you already have going on to attract visitors. Is your local GLBT community active in city affairs and politically influential, helping you to support the effort. Does the local GLBT community contribute to the city? In Dallas, the Dallas Tavern Guild not only creates events but enhances parks and other attributes of the destination. Identify your gay-friendly hotels. Get them excited about your efforts and the plan to bring them business as well. Be sure to ask if they are really gay-friendly or just in it for the business. Remember, gay travelers need to feel welcomed.

4. Bring your community together. Host a community leader breakfast, lunch, dinner or happy hour, anything! Invite all your local supporters in the community, anyone from city council, store owners, non-profits, chambers of commerce, pride coordinators, hotel representatives, local bar owners,

churches, whoever supports your GLBT community. Form a "City Ambassador Group" that will help you solicit, support, host, and perhaps, fund your efforts to attract more GLBT convention business. It's a great system when you have a strong group of 10–15 supporters. My advice is not to go it alone!

5. Education. This is a crucial step. You need to educate your community on how convention tourism affects them. Convention business brings economic rewards to nearly everyone in your city from the cab driver to the local bar, gay or straight. I like to tell my Dallas community that "EVERYBODY eats at the table." My main message is that if we all work together, we all make money, and then we all can give back. Remember, gay tourism is still considered controversial and there are many misunderstandings about this market. Trust me, I am a gal from Texas! There was lots of education that had to happen. To help keep a dialogue open, hold quarterly meetings to update your stakeholders with numbers and statistics that you compile. Show them the return on investment. Again, use business statistics every chance you get. Also, be sure to educate yourself by networking with colleagues in the tourism industry who are in the business of gay tourism.

6. Develop strategic alliances with major corporations in your city. Dallas has over 13 *Fortune* 500 companies in the city. More than half have a vice president of diversity and community relations and most major companies have gay employee groups who meet semi-regularly. Get to know those people! Major hotel chains have GLBT representatives. Get to know those people! There are also less obvious allies that can be very important to your efforts. These are people who may have resources, both financial and in-kind, that can help you achieve your goals. They can be local beer distributors, non-profit organizations, gay community groups, and gay bars and shops. Get to know these people!

7. Research all your local GLBT chapter associations and establish relationships with them. Develop a spreadsheet with every GLBT organization in your city from AIDS research centers to gay pride festival coordinators and black-tie dinner organizations. Find out who serves on the local boards of the Human Rights Campaign (HRC), Design Industries Fighting AIDS (DIFFA), Lavender Law and Servicemembers Legal Defense Network (SLDN), to name just a few. Make friends with these leaders and attend their events to support this

diverse community. Remember, these are the organizations that will work with you to organize their local conferences and meetings and pitch national conferences for your city as well.

8. Meet with national GLBT associations' convention planners. Most of the national associations have offices in Washington, D.C., and on the West Coast. Go to the Web and find out who they are. Almost every national GLBT association is listed. They all have national conventions. Get to know them. Stay organized and attend some of their trade shows. Any local tourism/convention tradeshows are always key to attend as well. Try to become key destination partners. Networking is key!

9. Host media and convention planner familiarization tours. Invite your clients, existing and potential, to see your city. Organize a three- or four-day trip with your local community supporters and show off your city and your hotels. Try to schedule this trip around the time of an annual GLBT event in your city to show off your gay pride. Many local pubs, restaurants, hotels and airlines would love to have the media visit their establishments. Publicity is a very important component in getting the word out about your destination's efforts.

10. Book the business by having a passion for what you do. It is not an easy market but it is a fun market. Support your community and have fun! It's not work when you love what you do! Lastly, stay informed by subscribing to all gay-related magazines and be sure to read your local "rags" because this is a fast-changing market. To book the business you must be aware of the opportunities and the issues in this community.

The role of gay marketing toward mainstream meetings and conventions

Ferguson advises that a destination should not limit its efforts to just the gay meetings and conventions. Members of the GLBT community are already participating in conventions regardless of the topic of the meeting. It may be a convention of real estate agents or dentists that will bring gay and straight attendees. Depending on the type of association you are hosting as a convention, gay and lesbian people can make up anywhere from a conservative 5 percent to more than 50 percent of the delegates.

Interestingly, GLBT leisure marketing and even some general market leisure campaigns placed in gay media campaigns do play an important role in influencing mainstream convention planners, especially those planners who are gay themselves. First and foremost, convention planners will first seek the best value and the best experience for their convention, according to Ferguson. Assuming your product fits the meeting planner's criteria and your city promotes itself as gay-friendly then you have the advantage because you will also have an appeal to the meeting planner's personal values.

Here are a few tips that mainstream convention planners could employ to increase registration to their convention and that can also make gay delegates feel at home:

- Provide a link from your organization's or convention website to the destination's gay-friendly website or local gay information.

- On convention registration forms, ask if they are bringing a domestic partner. If you don't ask you will never know and no one is forcing them to answer. Provide, upon request, a list of the local attractions of gay interest or gay nightlife.

- At the convention information desk, have a few Columbia Fun Maps for that city or destination for use upon request. Also, be sure your convention hotel concierge also has a few on hand.

Is there homophobia within conventions and meetings? Perhaps, and it does limit what becomes part of the official program for the convention. For associations and meeting planners to officially add gay and lesbian events to the mainstream program, GLBT members must become powerful enough and vocal enough within the organization to demand change. The challenge will always be making GLBT relevant to the organization's meeting. Cruise lines have begun offering a Friends of Dorothy networking meeting on ships. Could this idea be effective in mainstream meetings and conventions?

Gays and lesbians don't do buses but they do cruise

Gay tour operators are responding to a growing consumer trend of all-gay vacations on cruise ships, and in resorts and exotic adventure. Without question, the most popular form of group travel is the all-gay cruise vacation. Today, the most popular tour operators that cater exclusively to gay travelers are RSVP Vacations, R Family Vacations, Atlantis Vacations and Olivia Cruises and Resorts. Europe's largest gay tour operator is Man Around. There are also a number of smaller, boutique tour operators specializing in the gay and lesbian traveler such as Gay Asian Travel, Alternative Holidays (Europe), Rainbow Travel (Czech Republic), Absolute Sultans (Middle East), and Hermes Tours (Global). A great online resource is travelersdigest.com/gl.[5]

How big is the all-gay tour market? Enormous. RSVP Vacations predicts a 300 percent increase in sales for their all-gay cruise vacations before 2010. In fact, the company will charter the Queen Mary 2 in 2007.[6] RSVP has been in operation for more than 21 years. Founded in 1985, RSVP sets claim as the originator of the gay and lesbian cruise concept, and offers distinctive travel packages designed for gay and lesbian travelers. More than 80,000 men and women have participated in RSVP's big- and small-ship cruises, riverboat cruises, land tours, and resort vacations. They include the Caribbean, Central America, the Czech Republic, Austria, Hungary, Ireland, Mexico, French Polynesia, Peru and Thailand.

What is an all-gay cruise vacation like and how does a tour operator transform a mainstream cruise ship for the gay traveler? In March 2005, I took my first all-gay cruise vacation. I was a gay cruise virgin and there was no way I could write a book about gay tourism without seeing this first-hand. Embarking in the uber gay-friendly port of Ft. Lauderdale, I joined more than 2000 people on the Holland–America ship *MS. Westerdam* for an RSVP Vacation on a weeklong voyage through the Caribbean and to Mexico. The average age of an RSVP cruise guest seemed to be around 45 years and mostly male.

RSVP Vacations transformed the cruise experience, from the moment guests entered the Port Everglades Cruise Ship Terminal to the moment we departed a week later. First, gay tour operators conduct gay sensitivity training. RSVP brings in its own staff and customizes its own slate of main stage entertainment and creates themed parties. RSVP brought on board gay comedians, mainstream pop vocalists, including eighties icon Taylor Dayne. The themed parties are usually held each night on a dance floor that is especially erected on the back deck of the cruise ship complete with state-of-the-art sound and lighting. What does this cruise ship do differently than other traditional cruises? The typical high standards of service remain; however, cruise lines traditionally relax their rules about what constitutes formal night. Even then, on formal night at least 30 percent of the ship was dressed in tuxedos.

R Family Vacations
The Birth of the Family-Friendly, Gay-Friendly Vacations

Gregg Kaminsky, Co-founder[7]

R Family Vacations is the world's first successful family-friendly, gay-friendly vacation company. R Family Vacations was created for gay and lesbian travelers to see the world with their children, their friends and their parents. Before starting R Family Vacations with Rosie and Kelli O'Donnell in 2002, I was working for Atlantis Vacations, the largest all-gay vacation tour operator that was popular primarily with gay men. At Atlantis, we would charter the cruise ship and bring in musical artists, world-renowned DJs, celebrity comedians and other performers to entertain the guests.

Before I met my partner of seven years, Dan, he was great friends with Kelli Carpenter, who had not yet met television celebrity Rosie O'Donnell. Kelli met Rosie and then Dan met me about two years later. We all became friendly. At the time, I was still working for Atlantis Vacations, Rosie had her daytime television show, and Kelli was working at Nickelodeon as a marketing executive. Dan was an executive at Disney.

Over the next several years, Dan, Kelli, Rosie and I would always travel together with Rosie and Kelli's children. Their kids were always raised in an extremely open environment. They are definitely the kids of the future! These children don't know the difference between a gay couple and a straight couple. They just know love. If they see me alone they always ask, "Where's Dan?"

When I was still working at Atlantis Vacations, the superstar singing group En Vogue had to cancel their performance on an Atlantis Cruise just three days before the cruise was set to depart Miami with 2200 passengers. During this time, I had a very private relationship with Rosie and I had never asked her for anything professionally. This was the first time that I would call her to ask her to tap into her rolodex.

Rosie never really considered herself 'in the closet.' However, she was not totally out to the public and she still had her popular daytime talk show. It didn't occur to me to ask her to come on board to entertain. With no headliner still slated for this ship's departure, I called her and said, "you know every single celebrity, and I would never ask you for this but, is there someone you can call who would get on a plane in two days to go to Miami and perform on an all-gay cruise?"

Gregg Kaminsky and Kelli O'Donnell, co-founders of R Family Vacations (Courtesy of the Greater Philadelphia Tourism Marketing Corporation).

Rosie said, "how come you are not asking me to do it?" I was surprised by her response because this was right before the Diane Sawyer ABC prime-time interview where she would tell the world that she was lesbian, in a relationship with Kelli and living with their children. Why would I think she would come on an all-gay cruise?

To my delight and surprise, she and Kelli decided to come on the cruise. Of course, the gay boys loved her but what they didn't know is that this cruise would change Rosie's life and mine. Until the Atlantis cruise Rosie had no idea how important a gay vacation was or what the experience was like when people were surrounded by people just like themselves. She saw first-hand that a place could be created that is free of judgment and where you do not have to compromise your lifestyle. When two men or two women go on vacation, you shouldn't be asked if you want a king bed or two double beds, you know what I mean? No one should assume you are just friends. She left that trip so blown away.

Rosie finally made her first visit to Provincetown when Kelli was expecting their fourth child and they wanted to have a quiet weekend away. By total coincidence it happened to be Women's Week. Kelli and Rosie were walking down Commercial Street with thousands of women. She thinks it was like gay Disney

World. Rosie called me and said she wanted to take Dan, me and the kids on one of those gay cruises. I said, "Rosie there is Olivia cruises, but that is exclusively women. You can come on Atlantis or RSVP but the kids can't come." A little light bulb went off.

By this time, Kelli left Nickelodeon to stay at home with their four children. She was itching to do something. With Kelli's marketing experience, my travel background, and our amazing friendship, we are a great team. Rosie gave us the go-ahead and the backing to create R Family Vacations.

R Family has been the most incredible journey for me. In 2003, we started a meeting with all the cruise lines. I had no idea what it was going to feel like or what the trips would feel like. I had no idea that people would show up. The first year was a struggle. I wanted to start small and then grow into a larger cruise ship. Rosie has this theory that you "go big or go home." She wanted a big new cruise ship and assured me that if we make a bold statement it will grow much more quickly in a few years. We had 1600 people on the first cruise that could have held 2200 passengers. The cruise was a really diverse group of people. We had gays and lesbians, gays and lesbian parents, aunts, uncles, grandparents, children of gays and lesbians, parents of gays and lesbians and friends of gays and lesbians. Also, there were many gays and lesbians who were seeking an alternative to some of the party-intense events in our community and our cruise was a wonderful option.

In 2005, we had 2100 people on board. In 2006, 2800 people sailed with R Family Vacations and we had to turn people away at the dock. As usual, Rosie was right.

We have come a long way since our first cruise. We now have an official airline partner, American Airlines. HBO shot an Emmy-nominated documentary about our company. We also have a very loyal customer base that continues to grow each year. In addition to our vacations, we have created an online community on our website, rfamilyvacations.com, where information can be shared and people can book a future vacation. In 2007, we will sail with two full ships plus we had our first land-based R Family Vacation in Philadelphia.

Notes

1. GFN. com (Source: Associated Press), Texas Maybe Homophobic But Not Dallas, November 11, 2006.
2. Ferguson, Jack P., senior vice president, Philadelphia Convention & Visitors Bureau, in-person interview, October 27, 2006.
3. Community Marketing Inc., San Francisco, California, October 2006.

4. Torres, Veronica, Diversity Convention Sales Manager, Dallas Convention & Visitors Bureau, written by source, July 2006.
5. Traveler's Digest, Gay and Lesbian Travel Directory, www.travelersdigest.com, November 2006.
6. Brenna, Pat, RSVP Vacations, onboard MS Westerdam, Travel Agent Reception, February 2006.
7. Kaminsky, Gregg, Co-Founder, R Family Vacations, in-person interview, September 7, 2006.

CHAPTER 8

Gay sports: an international marketing tool

In Montreal in July 2006, Tom Roth from Community Marketing, Jeff Marsh from Orbitz and I were there for the opening ceremonies of the 1st World Outgames. Using facilities originally built for the Montreal XXI Olympiad in 1976, 12,000 athletes from nearly 100 countries were joined by 40,000 spectators who cheered as Olympian Mark Tewksbury and tennis legend Martina Navratilova took to the elaborate stage. With the Canadian Broadcasting Corporation (CBC) broadcasting live nationally, gay tourism history was made (yet again!) And, we were there.

By most newspaper accounts up to 500,000 people over the span of nearly two weeks came to Montreal and they spent money. For eleven days, Montreal was host to a major international event combining sport, culture and human rights. The International Conference on Lesbian, Gay, Bisexual and Transgender (LGBT) Human Rights from 26 to 29 July brought together 1516 participants from every corner of the globe to discuss the worldwide situation of LGBT people. The 35 sport disciplines of the 1st World Outgames drew 10,248 athletes, while 835 people came together for the cultural component of the program. It also took 110 employees, 5200 volunteers, 306 organizing committee members,

494 officials and over one hundred suppliers, to oversee the competitions, performances, ceremonies and over one hundred other events and activities that made up the 11-day international event.[1]

Gay sporting events and competitions are one of the most lucrative and untapped areas of gay tourism. Gay sports enthusiasts are gay travelers. They travel for regional, national, continental and international sports competitions, and the gay sporting competitions generate millions of dollars for local economies.[2,3]

Tourism professionals looking to increase business in the short term would be wise to invest resources toward the gay sports market to position their destination for long-term growth. Sporting competition means big business for the tourism industry. Cities around the world spend billions to host the Olympics in an effort to put their destination on the map. Cities like Atlanta, Sydney, Torino, Mexico City and Seoul have all successfully used the Olympics to pump millions of dollars into the local economy;[4] generate national and international recognition for the host city through extensive media exposure; and to rally the local community toward one common vision.

The funny thing about gay-friendly sports is that you can accomplish some of the same goals as you want to do with other international sporting events, such as the Olympics. With one big exception – it will cost you much less to do it.

Every athlete, tourist and Canadian resident at the 1st World Outgames had one thing in common: they responded to marketing. Why is it so efficient to market to gay people internationally? The GLBT community is perhaps the most wired community in the world![7] It is efficient and affordable to reach amateur gay sporting enthusiasts around the globe, especially when compared to the mainstream market. Think about it. How much money would it take to launch a traditional global marketing campaign to entice 12,000 people plus 500,000 spectators from 100 countries to your destination at a specific time of year? If you were presenting a marketing plan to your CEO and said that you need to reach people who live in more than 100 countries and you want them to visit and sleep over in hotels for nearly a week, how much money do you think it would take?

The 1st World Outgames reported a total marketing budget valued at $13 million, (Canadian) with an initial $5.3 million spent for marketing and a staff of ten out of a total organizational budget of $16 million.[8] The media partnerships that were created by the organizers of the 1st World Outgames brought the Montreal message to 4 million people in over 80 countries and the organizer's website averaged 300,000 hits per month and their newsletter had a subscriber base of 75,000 people.[9] The 1st

World Outgames was funded with 33 percent coming from public funds; 29 percent coming from earned revenue; 22 percent from corporate sponsorships; and 15 percent from other earned revenue.[10]

Gay sports remains an emerging growth market as evidenced by the increasing number of sporting competitions and the steady growth in attendance at those events by athletes and spectators alike. Corporate investment through sponsorships and support is just beginning and will continue to grow at an extraordinary pace. More investment will help to make staging a global sporting event even more affordable and attainable for destinations everywhere.

There are regional gay sporting competitions that are held annually; multi-country competitions in Europe and North America held semi-annually; and two worldwide sporting competitions, modeled after the Olympics, held every four years with participants from more than 100 countries, called the Gay Games and the World Outgames.

There are two international gay sporting organizations, the Federation of Gay Games (FGG)[11] and the Gay and Lesbian International Sports Association (GLISA).[12] Both the Federation of Gay Games and GLISA are made up of individual organizations that represent athletic organizations from six continents. The Federation of Gay Games licenses the Gay Games to a host city. The Gay Games is eight days of sports competitions, arts and culture, and social events. The Outgames licenses the World Outgames to a host city. The World Outgames is ten days of sport, culture, business and international conference programs. In 2006, Chicago was host to the Gay Games VII and Montreal was host to the 1st World Outgames. Now held in opposite years, Cologne will host the Gay Games VII in 2010 and Copenhagen will host the 2nd World Outgames in 2009.

Gay sporting competitions include badminton, basketball, beach volleyball, bowling, cycling, cross-country, dance sport, darts, diving, dragon boat regatta, figure skating, flag football, gold, handball, ice hockey, karate, marathon, marital arts, physique, pool billiards, power lifting, racquetball, road races, roller racing, rowing, rugby, sailing, soccer, football, softball, squash, swimming, synchronized swimming, table tennis, tennis, track and field, triathlon, volleyball, water polo and wrestling.

Hosting the Gay Games or the World Outgames means big business for the local hospitality industry. Each event attracts hundreds of thousands of spectators over the span of events, including athletes and media from around the world. The international sporting competitions generate nearly $75 million in direct economic impact. Since these are the largest sporting events with the most opportunity for marketers, this chapter will focus primarily on these events.

How big is the gay sports movement? Simply put, enormous. Since the 1990s, GLBT sports movement has grown significantly and so have the substantial economic rewards. Consider these facts:[13]

- Since 1994, each Gay Games has drawn an average of more than 12,000 participants. That is comparable to the Summer Olympics.

- The 1998 Gay Games in Amsterdam drew an estimated 250,000 spectators. In 1994, in New York during the Stonewall Celebration, the Games drew more than 500,000 spectators.

- Amsterdam estimated its tourism windfall for Gay Games V at $55 million. Sydney's Gay Games VI had an estimated impact of $60 million.

Charles Lapointe, president and CEO of Tourisme Montréal, emphasized the important economic and tourism repercussions of the event in a press release prior to the Out Games. "The 250,000 visitors expected represent more than 171 million dollars that will be generated by 1st World Outgames. It will also further enhance Montréal's image as a gay destination par excellence. Montréal is known around the world for its spirit of openness and respect."[14]

Why are gay sporting competitions necessary?

The first question I always have heard is, why do gay people need their own sporting competition? Well, if you read Mark Tweksbury's 2006 book *Inside Out: Straight Talk from a Gay Jock*, he tells you that the world of sport is a world of uber masculinity. Professional sport does not nurture gay athletes.[5] Combine that with the fact that there is a long list of countries in the world that still imprison or kill people if they openly acknowledge that they are GLBT.[6] The world of gay sport is a way to compete in a safe, open and, by the way, festival atmosphere free of discrimination or fear.

The most frequently asked question is, why in the world would you need a gay Olympic-style competition? The key difference between the Olympics and gay sports is that being gay, lesbian, bisexual or transgenered comes with political, social and religious consequences at home and in the world of sports. Gay athletes are oftentimes not "out" at home, at work, in sport or to their families. How many "out" gay professional or amateur gay athletes can you name? Gay sports present athletes the opportunity to express themselves openly, to experience the camaraderie of GLBT people

Event	Host City	Year	Athletes
Gay Games I	San Francisco	1982	1,350
Gay Games II	San Francisco	1986	3,500
Gay Games III	Vancouver	1990	7,300
Gay Games IV	New York	1994	12,500
Gay Games V	Amsterdam	1998	13,000
Gay Games VI	Sydney	2002	11,000
Gay Games VII	Chicago	2006	12,000*
1st World Outgames	Montreal	2006	12,000*

(*estimated)

from around the world and earn validation through striving for a personal best in an inclusive environment.[15]

The Gay Games, which held its first competition in 1982, was conceived as a "vehicle of change" in 1980 by founder Dr. Tom Waddell and a group of San Francisco residents, including Mark Brown and Paul Mart. Dr. Waddell, a 1968 Olympic decathlete, dreamed of a sporting event based on the philosophy that "doing one's personal best should be the paramount goal in any athletic endeavor."[16]

"The Gay Games are not separatist, they are not exclusive, they are not oriented to victory, and they are not for commercial gain," Waddell wrote after the first Gay Games according to the FGG. "They intended to bring a global community together in friendship, to experience participation, to elevate consciousness and self-esteem, and to achieve a form of cultural and intellectual synergy. We have the opportunity to take the initiative on critical issues that affect the quality of life."

Gay Games I and II were produced by the San Francisco Arts & Athletics (SFAA). Tom Waddell lost his battle with AIDS and died in July 1987, less than a year after Gay Games II, but his legacy was assured as the inspiration for future Gay Games. The SFAA board of directors, which included Tom's widow Sara Waddell Lewinstein, took steps to enlarge its membership beyond the Bay Area and in 1989 changed its name to the Federation of Gay Games.

The FGG describes the organization today as one with a mission to ensure that GLBT athletes and friends have the chance to engage in sports in a safe and supportive environment which preserves rights, dignity and respect. The FGG works to increase the involvement of women, seniors, transgendered and persons at all levels and in all functions and roles in sports and sport organization. The FGG works to ensure that the knowledge, experience and values of the GLBT community contribute to the development of sport in this community and in the mainstream sport community. The FGG sees itself as values driven rather than just event driven.

Founded in 2004 over an ideological debate over the future of the global GLBT sports movement between the FGG and the 2006 host city committee in Montreal, Canada, GLISA is a new international sports organization dedicated to developing gay and lesbian sport worldwide.[17]

Here is a little history on what led to the creation of two international sporting organizations. In 2001, the Federation of Gay Games selected Montreal to host the 2006 Gay Games. However, by November 2003 a contract was still unsigned as Montreal organizers and the FGG were deadlocked in disagreements over the control and scope of the event. Eventually, the Montreal organizers decided to walk away from further negotiations and, on November 9, 2003, announced that they would stage their own event autonomous from the FGG. First called Rendez-Vous Montreal 2006, the event was later renamed Outgames after the formation of GLISA in January 2004. Meanwhile the FGG chose Chicago as the new host of the 2006 Gay Games.

Marketing to gay consumers through gay sports

Gay sport teams are highly organized, yet very difficult to reach through traditional marketing programs. Because many of the organizers are volunteers, the travel industry cannot rely on the traditional marketing mix to reach potential visitors. However, there are easy and affordable non-traditional marketing techniques to reach these grassroots organizations.
Here are a few tips:

- The first step is to identify what gay sporting competitions your sporting venues can host. By narrowing your field, your outreach efforts can be highly efficient.

- Get online. The Web is filled with information on gay sporting events and oftentimes, you will find a person to contact about organizing an event.

- Next, engage your local gay sporting organizations to make connections with organizers of sports competitions.

- The best form of advertising is to make a commitment to sponsor your local gay sporting teams and, then, the competitive events in your key feeder markets.

- Go to where the athletes are. Exhibit with a table or a booth at the Gay Games, the World Outgames, the EuroGames or at nearby sporting competitions.

- Invest in the Web. Gay athletes are highly wired. Competitions are organized online. Provide content about your destination and sponsor gay sport websites.

- Don't forget to use your traditional gay tourism advertising and media relations. In your cooperative advertising, call out that your destination is gay-sports friendly. Consider hosting a press trip with a gay sports theme.

American companies are increasingly using gay sport to market their products or services to gay and lesbian consumers. Increasingly, the stigma toward marketing to the gay consumer is vanishing. American companies are no longer "marketing" in the closet and even more importantly, they are taking a stand against groups who threaten boycotts or negative publicity.[18]

The host committees of the Gay Games VII and the 1st World Outgames were extraordinarily successful in securing mainstream corporate sponsorship. Chicago secured sponsorships from Chicago-based Exelon Corporation, Walgreens, RCN Cable, Altoids®, Kraft, Amtrak and others.[19]

Montreal 2006 secured a total of 14 million dollars in cash, goods or services from the Governments of Canada and of Québec, the City of Montréal, Labatt beer, Bell Canada Enterprises and 40 media partners.[20]

While cash, as they say, will always be king (or queen in this instance), getting the word out about the events to athletes and spectators around the world played a vital role. Both Montreal and Chicago forged cross-promotional partnerships with professional, sport and other types of associations to promote the games. Below are a few examples of how the companies negotiated marketing deals that were a win-win for both the gay sporting competitions and for their sponsoring companies.

The following were the sponsors of the Gay Games in Chicago:[21]

Orbitz was named the official online travel agency for Gay Games VII. As a Global Gold Sponsor, Orbitz provided travel and lodging services to the Chicago organizers of the Gay Games and promoted the Gay Games in Orbitz television ads on Bravo and other networks. Special Chicago destination information and promotion of the Gay Games and Orbitz travel services were distributed online to millions of lesbian, gay, bisexual and transgender people worldwide.

California-based Q Television Network won the gay network television, radio and Internet broadcast rights in a deal with the Gay Games VII valued at more than $3.2 million, $1.7 million in cash plus $1.5 million in advertising and programming benefits. This network ran into financial challenges prior to the Gay Games and it is unclear how much of this sponsorship was actually realized.

PlanetOut Inc., online global media company, became a Gay Games VII Premium Sponsor in a deal valued around $1 million. Gay Games VII were promoted to PlanetOut's 3.3 million active members residing in more than 100 countries throughout the world, including sites specifically serving the GLBT communities of Argentina, Australia, Brazil, France, Germany, Italy, Mexico, Spain, USA (both English and Spanish) and the United Kingdom.

Centaur Music partnered with the Chicago Gay Games, making Centaur the official music sponsor. Centaur produced two official CDs for the Chicago Gay Games, including a new dance mix entitled "Gay Games Chicago 2006," mixed by XM satellite radio jock Joe Bermudez, who is well known for his smash-hit radio mixes for Kelly Clarkson, Shakira and Jessica Simpson. "Gay Games Chicago 2006" CD hit music was sold in stores throughout the United States.

For the 1st World Outgames,[22] Speedo created a special athletic collection carrying the World Outgames insignia. Mikasa, known worldwide for its athletic balls used in Olympic Games and various world championships, was the official supplier of athletic balls in the basketball, volleyball, handball, beach volleyball, soccer and water polo events of the 1st World Outgames.

Other sporting events

The EuroGames, the European Gay and Lesbian Sports Championships, attracts 5000 registered competitors in 26 sports. The EuroGames, Europe's largest gay sporting event, has been held each summer since 1992 except in years in which Gay Games were held. In 2008, the EuroGames will be held in Barcelona, Spain.[23]

The Gay Softball World Series brings 150 teams from the United States and Canada for a week-long competition. The 30th Annual Gay Softball World Series was held in Ft. Lauderdale, Florida, in 2006.[24]

The Gay and Lesbian Tennis Alliance is an international organization, comprised of 40 gay and lesbian tennis clubs with 5500 players. The alliance manages and sanctions the gay tennis circuit with 39 annual GLTA-sanctioned tournaments in the United States, Canada and Europe.[25]

The International Gay Rugby Association and Board (IGRAB) has U.S. teams in San Francisco, Washington, D.C., Chicago, Phoenix, Portland, San Diego and European teams in Denmark, Sweden, France, London and Wales. The IGRAB hosts an international rugby competition, the Bingham Cup, named in honor of Mark Kendall Bingham, a victim of September 11. The first Bingham Cup was held in 2002 in San Francisco. That year, eight teams traveled to California to compete over two days. In 2004, the Bingham Cup was held in London but now with 20 teams from four countries. New York City hosted the 2006 Bingham Cup.[26]

The International Gay Rodeo Association (IGRA) is an organization comprised of numerous regional Gay Rodeo Associations from across the United States and Canada. IGRA-sanctioned rodeos are hosted by local associations each year and culminate in an IGRA Finals Rodeo where the top 20 contestants in each event compete for the title of IGRA International Champion. The 30th anniversary of the IGRA Finals Rodeo was held in Reno, Nevada. Most interestingly, destinations that promote themselves as gay-friendly, such as Ft. Lauderdale, show greater attendance.[27]

Staying on top of the world of gay sports

A resource to become educated on the world of gay sports, in addition to websites of the FGG and GLISA, is Outsports.com. Outsports.com offers a mixture of breaking news, commentary, features, member profiles, photo galleries and discussion boards. Outsports' mission is to offer the gay sports community the broadest, deepest, most-informative and most-entertaining website. Outsports.com was founded in 2000 by Jim Buzinski and Cyd Zeigler, Jr.

Case study

Montreal, Canada

The Honorable Charles Lapointe[28]
Chairman of the Canadian Tourism Commission
President and Chief Executive Officer, Greater Montreal Convention and Tourism Bureau

As a marketer, I always have my eyes focused on what will bring more tourists to Montreal. It is my job to understand the

Tourism Montreal's advertising is sexy, exciting and diverse.

destination's strengths, weaknesses and potential. Back in 1992, I noticed a revival in the gay village in Montreal (Le Village gai). This area of Montreal was developing a proper mix of shops, bars and a joyful atmosphere on the street that was very appealing. I recognized early on that Montreal was naturally developing a strong product that would appeal to gay tourists.

I asked my staff to find all the networks in the gay travel business where we could identify resources and potential business for the city. Parallel to this industry research, I decided to become more familiar with the local gay community. I wanted to identify the influencers and leaders in this community. To my delight I found an active gay community who were willing to work with the bureau to make Montreal one of the greatest gay-friendly destinations in the world. At this time, there was not a gay chamber of commerce or organization; however, within three years' time, one would be created.

After nearly 18 months of gathering data on this market, I presented my analysis to my board. With their support, we agreed that gay tourism represented a good market for us. Our first step was to create a long-term strategy. In 1996, I earmarked $125,000 (Canadian), which included money for research with Community Marketing Inc. in San Francisco. We educated two of our employees in gay and lesbian tourism, one in the leisure market and one in media relations. We kept a dialogue going with the local gay community and we asked them to help Tourism Montreal draw up a list of all major events in leisure, sports, contests and conventions. The sales team created client profiles and later that year, Tourism Montreal launched our first leisure marketing campaign. Our publicity staff identified influential media in the United States, Canada and Europe and we also hosted our first gay press trip. Since then, we regularly host two gay press trips per year.

Today, the local gay community is very strong and organized. Each year the gay chamber produces the gay city guide. It is financed by Tourism Montreal but it is the chamber's responsibility to produce it. Tourism Montreal also believes in supporting other efforts of the local GLBT community, especially with those events that are proven to drive tourism to Montreal. Each year, we provide financial support for major gay events like Black and Blue, organized by the BBCM Foundations, and Divers/cite. We think it is important for Montreal's nightlife to be seen on par with the big circuit parties in cities like South Beach, Florida.

We have had a long partnership with Tourism Quebec, who have helped us regionalize our gay marketing program. In 2006, the Canadian Tourism Commission announced a $300,000 gay tourism campaign, which allows other Canadian cities, including Toronto and Vancouver, to work with Tourism Quebec and Tourism Montreal to position Canada as a gay-friendly country.

Our efforts have paid off. In 1998, Montreal was host to the International Gay and Lesbian Tourism Association, and in 2007, we will host IGLTA again. Montreal has welcomed Gay and Lesbian Association of Choruses in 2004, and in 2006, Montreal was host to the 1st World Outgames, which drew more than 500,000 participants to the city. Since 1993, Tourism Montreal has invested $2 million (CAD) toward gay travel. Montreal welcomes 400,000 gay and lesbian tourists annually and they spend more than $250 million.

The future of gay tourism is very bright. I think there will always be a need for the gay community to regularly get together. While gay tourism is developing at a rapid pace in the United States, Europe and Canada, it is not yet a worldwide phenomenon. Globally there is still room to grow.

Notes

1. Verikios, Michael, *Travel Daily News*, The First World Outgames Montreal Welcomed Half A Million Spectators, August 9, 2006.
2. The Federation of Gay Games, www.gaygames.com.
3. The Gay and Lesbian International Sporting Association, www.glisa.org.
4. Price Waterhouse Coopers, European Economic Outlook, June 2004.
5. Tewksbury, Mark, *Inside Out*, Wiley, 2006.
6. Amnesty International, Sexual Minorities and the Law: A World Survey, 2006, www.ailgbt.org, November 2006.
7. Gay and Lesbian Tourism Profile 2006, Community Marketing, Inc. San Francisco, CA, October 2006.
8. Gay and Lesbian International Sporting Association, Activity Report to GLISA Inaugural Delegate Congress, August 30–Setember 2, 2005.
9. Tewksbury, Mark, Address to Metropolitan Montreal Board of Trade, March 23, 2006.
10. Tewksbury, Mark, Address to Metropolitan Montreal Board of Trade, March 23, 2006.
11. The Federation of Gay Games, www.gaygames.com.
12. The Gay and Lesbian International Sporting Association, www.glisa.org.
13. The Federation of Gay Games, www.gaygames.com.
14. The Gay and Lesbian International Sporting Association, www.glisa.org.
15. Tewksbury, Mark, *Inside Out*, Wiley, 2006.
16. The Federation of Gay Games, www.gaygames.com.
17. Tewksbury, Mark, *Inside Out*, Wiley, 2006.
18. Editorial, Advertising Age, A Vote Against Discrimination, April 3, 2006.
19. The Federation of Gay Games, www.gaygames.com.
20. The Gay and Lesbian International Sporting Association, www.glisa.org.
21. The Federation of Gay Games, www.gaygames.com.
22. The Gay and Lesbian International Sporting Association, www.glisa.org.
23. The European Gay and Lesbian Sports Championships, www.eurogames.info.
24. The North American Gay Amateur Athletic Association, www.nagaaasoftball.org.

25. The Gay and Lesbian Tennis Alliance, www.glta.net.
26. International Gay Ruby Association and Board, www.igrab.net.
27. International Gay Rodeo Association, www.igra.com.
28. Lapointe, Honorable Charles, Chairman of the Canadian Tourism Commission. President and Chief Executive Officer, Greater Montreal Convention and Tourism Bureau, phone interview, October 6, 2006.

The future

In October 2006, gay tourism "officially arrived" when the Travel Industry of America (TIA) bestowed its highest honor, the Domestic See America Marketing Odessey Award, on Philadelphia's gay tourism campaign. In front of the entire travel industry, TIA declared 2006 the year of the gay traveler. This award was a signal that gay tourism had officially come out of the closet and was a market segment that was as relevant and as important as any other. What was perhaps most significant about winning this award was that it beat out award entries from around the world in a mainstream category. Until this time, most awards for gay and lesbian tourism marketing were won in the multicultural award categories. By December 2006, TIA unveiled the results from its first ever GLBT research study.

Now that TIA and other world travel organizations have "sanctioned" gay tourism, you will see more destinations; transportation companies, cruise companies and others proudly come out to make an invitation to the gay traveler. The future of gay and lesbian tourism is very exciting. Only a few years ago, gay tourism was limited to just a few out-of-the way destinations. Gay travelers were relegated to the "known" gay destinations. Today, the competition for the lucrative gay travel market is fierce and it will continue. Gay travel is still in an extraordinary growth phase.

Gay travelers will always need a special invitation because they aren't always sure if they are welcomed or invited to visit. There will always be a need to place relevant images paired with appropriate messages in the media which GLBT people are

The future is freedom to market to gay and lesbian travel (Courtesy of Greater Philadelphia Tourism Marketing Corporation).

using to make travel decisions. However, what you will see is more mainstream cross-over.

Very soon, there will be few barriers still left to break. There will be fewer press releases that can credibly say "first," "never before" or "ground-breaking" when it comes to gay tourism. However, there is a decade of innovation still ahead of us.

Further, simply "coming out" as gay-friendly no longer assures you a spot on the list of favorite gay destinations or travel companies. In fact, gay travelers already expect you to be gay-friendly, so announcing it no longer gets you points. Smart marketers will combine entry into the gay and lesbian travel market with a demonstration of good intent and a sophisticated knowledge of what their product has to specifically offer the GLBT traveler.

Here are my predictions for the future:

- Icons that indicate gay-friendly (Rainbow Flag, IGLTA logo) will be more prominently displayed in all marketing materials including websites and brochures. Travel companies and destinations will no longer hide the GLBT information but give it relevant placement alongside other information.

- Gay tourism will become less controversial and more accepted among stakeholders and the public. Travel companies will be less afraid of alienating current customers by marketing to GLBT travelers. In fact, the gay and lesbian market will become a part of most tourism marketing campaigns.

- More mainstream travel publications and newspaper travel sections and websites that have travel sections will include GLBT travel information, making GLBT travel information more accessible to a wider audience.

- Gay and lesbian media companies (i.e. Planet Out, LPI Media and Viacom) will continue to grow in reach and advertising revenue. More of us will be advertising with gay media and more people will be subscribing to gay media outlets. This will mean that marketers will have to dedicate more of their budgets to reach GLBT travelers.

- The United States will catch up to Europe and Canada, where GLBT are a part of the expected experience in the destination and included as a market segment like any other, including African American, Hispanic, and so on.

- Gay and lesbian travelers will be offered more travel choices at better prices as more places and companies compete for their discretionary dollars. This will mean that the travel "product" will have to be more thoroughly refined and defined.

- Corporations will continue to invest marketing dollars into local GLBT events, such as pride festivals and gay sporting competitions, at a new level. This will result in bringing more financial resources to the GLBT community, who will in return produce better events that will expose more people to the product or service. This is perhaps the most exciting development on the horizon.

- The gay travel market will be better researched, leading to better understanding of the market, which will in turn allow marketers to more effectively deploy resources, construct more relevant messages and more fully measure the return on investment.

- Advertising will mature. Destinations and travel companies will be less fearful of showing two same-sex couples holding hands or in intimate situations, such as when selling a romantic weekend. Today, there remains a hesitation to show same-sex couples present in opposite-sex couple situations (e.g., a luxurious room with room service overlooking a beautiful beach).

- The GLBT community will go mainstream yet demand and expect gay amenities. This means that gay travelers will expect that you have a Friends of Dorothy social gathering on board every cruise ship sailing or that you always have in-room entertainment and movies that are of gay interest. Gays and lesbians will be increasingly accepted as a part of the fold and not the fringe.

- The competition for GLBT meetings, conventions and sporting competitions will catch up to its mainstream counterparts. Destinations will have to "invest" in luring the most coveted business to their destination.

Destinations too will have to develop their gay brand. You will see the best gay beach destinations, best places for lesbians, top European cities for gay men and even adventure travel. What kind of gay traveler would like to visit your destination? The gay outdoor market will be perhaps the largest growth market that tourism has ever seen. Masculine adventure activities such as hiking, biking and rowing are not often associated with gay men or lesbians.

You will also see travel companies brand their product very distinctly. Olivia Vacations is clearly moving toward the lesbian traveler willing to pay a premium for the best in lesbian vacations. Olivia's move to the super luxury lesbian market will lead to a large void in the gay travel market that will be filled by another gay tour operator who will serve the mid-level lesbian market. Planet Out's RSVP Vacations is working hard to fill that gap.

You will have super luxury gay cruise and tour operators like Olivia Vacations, who are investing in A-list celebrities like Whoopi Goldberg to perform in their cruises to ensure their position as a market leader. International superstar Gloria Estefan performed onboard an R Family Vacation cruise in February 2007, and she will not be the last mega star to entertain the gay traveler.

Most experts featured in this book agree that the next frontier in gay travel is the lesbian traveler. Gay marketing and research have primarily been geared toward gay men. You will see a significant rise in the marketing toward lesbians and they will become another way in which destinations define themselves. There is a race currently going on to create a top-10 list of destinations for lesbians. According to research commissioned by Philadelphia in 2005,[1] Provincetown was rated the number one U.S. destination for lesbians. After Provincetown, there was no other U.S. destination that was cited as strong number two.

Miami has been gaining a reputation as a lesbian-friendly destination primarily through an event called Aqua Girl, which began as a one-day event in 1999 and now is one of the preeminent lesbian fundraising events that last several days. Girls Gay Days and Girls in Wonderland Disney are increasingly attracting more lesbians to the annual Gay Days events.

More marketers have realized the potential in the lesbian market. In 2006, Philadelphia unofficially launched "the year of the lesbian traveler." More advertising dollars were allocated to lesbian magazines; the destination took out its first ad in *Damron Women's Traveller*, a guide book, added more lesbian-oriented content to gophila.com/gay and began sponsoring events that attracted lesbians. Other destinations including Miami, Key West and Washington, D.C., also employ specific marketing strategies for lesbians.

On the other hand, some very respected and knowledgeable leaders in gay tourism in Europe have argued that all-gay vacations will disappear as gay people become more accepted in society and can travel "openly." Others predict the market will grow not decline because there are so many areas of the world left to be discovered.

Mark Elderkin, Founder, Gay.com, sees the future in these four categories:[2]

1. Gay diversity marketing

2. Gay business travel

3. Gay family travel

4. All-gay cruise travel

Mark Elderkin also said that "The travel industry has been at the forefront of the gay market. Now, consumer package goods, the automotive industry and other industries have to catch up."

Richard Grey said in a *Passport* magazine interview said that "Travel has evolved." Grey offered this perspective, "Ten years ago gays would look for all-gay properties just because they were in the closet and it was a better opportunity to meet someone. There's a new trend in gay travel which is mainstream. There will always be a need for all gay accommodations... but we're definitely moving towards mainstream."[3]

Robert Witeck sees the future as, "Gay youth who shun labels. Gay marketing will take on a new identity. It will be inclusive and not uber gay. For example, Logo chose the name "logo" so it couldn't be labeled. Logo means Identity. Gay will grow to new categories outside of travel."[4]

As the cost of gay media increases, there will be a need to increase gay tourism marketing budgets to remain competitive. There may come a time when gay-friendly destinations themselves begin a cooperative advertising program between non-competing gay-friendly destinations. Richard Grey has been advocating this concept for many years now. The challenge is essentially creative. How do you market two or more destinations in one full-page ad? I feel confident that someone will figure it out.

George and Betty at American Airlines say that the competition will grow in the future as more companies pay closer attention to the economics of the gay traveler. Those who were the first to market will always have that halo effect and the years of goodwill that has been built up in the community. They think that marketers will have to constantly be thinking about what's next and how to make your product better. George and Betty also say that with a whole new generation of gay people growing up and becoming consumers, they will need to be educated on what companies have already done to win their business. To help build loyalty among the young GLBT generation, American Airlines are supporters of GLBT community centers, which is a very smart marketing move since community centers tend to attract the younger GLBT set. Community centers tend to be gathering places for younger members of the GLBT community. American Airlines wants younger GLBT people to grow up hearing American Airlines.[5]

They also see an extraordinary rise in the business traveler sector. Gay-owned businesses are a new market that is becoming increasingly easier to identify and to market to because of the creation of the National Gay and Lesbian Chamber of Commerce. In addition, strategic alliances with local gay and lesbian chambers in primary markets will reinforce the national effort.

Expert soapbox

Trends in GLBT tourism

Thomas Roth, founder and president[6]
Community Marketing, Incorporated

Gay and Lesbian tourism marketing is a dynamic industry. Here are the eight top trends that will impact the future of gay tourism marketing:

1. The end of "Pink Washing." Community Marketing coined this term for companies that are explicitly marketing to the GLBT community with ads and promotions, but at the same time are fighting against internal employee equality or are supporting anti-gay causes. These companies slap a rainbow on their ads, and expect the three-dollar-bills to flow. They are putting on a thin gay-friendly veneer, but there is no substance behind it. More aware gay and lesbian consumers are voting with their wallets. Consumers are aware of the HRC Equality Index when choosing a company to buy from, or work for. Travelers are selecting qualified TAG Approved hotels and resorts, known for their gay-progressive best practices. They are choosing to visit destinations that are making outreach, while ensuring that vacation experience is genuinely welcoming for all, including the gay community.

2. Diversification and stratification. Only a decade ago, gay and lesbian travelers had few destinations where they could feel genuinely welcome. Among them were the gay Meccas of Key West, Provincetown, Palm Springs, San Francisco and Amsterdam. As the appeal of "the gay market" has grown, largely due to market research findings, more destinations are including the gay community in their outreach plans. Notable among them (but not a complete list) are Philadelphia, Dallas, Seattle and even Bloomington, Indiana. What this means to gay and lesbian travelers is a broader diversity of destination options, reflecting the broad diversity of our community. More "regional destinations" on the gay map, such as Philadelphia and Dallas, become magnets for weekend getaways and extended business trips. And increased variety of art, music, culinary and architectural offerings, as well as Pride and other events, fit the bill for our community's many cultural interests.

3. LGBT tourism as activism. As a viable and favorable side-effect of tourism marketing, destinations are making a difference for

their own citizens. Destinations are looking at their own laws and social policies to evaluate whether they are genuinely "gay-friendly," and if they find weaknesses, they are initiating positive change. That may mean a city government including sexual orientation in their equal hiring practices, or it may mean a company sourcing gay vendors when making purchases. It may mean support or sponsorship of an GLBT charity event. With more awareness of the fact that these behind-the-scenes changes are meaningful motivators for gay travelers considering a destination or travel purchase, these marketers are investing in good corporate citizenship as a foundation for success in the market. This trend benefits travelers, of course, but even more it benefits the citizens of those cities, or the employees of that organization. Another example of GLBT tourism as activism is the reality that when gay vacationers visit a destination, they enjoy meeting locals. Sharing experiences, ideas and successes in the fight for GLBT equality empowers those local citizens, and ultimately increases the possibility of better lives for all gay and lesbian citizens. Vacationers are also "ambassadors" when visiting places with few visible gay and lesbian citizens. More mingling with locals who may have stereotyped views of our community sensitizes them that we are "people, too," opens awareness, and ultimately decreases fear and resulting hostility.

4. Destination marketers become "gay aggressive." Perhaps the most striking trend is in terms of how actively destinations are presenting themselves to the community. A decade ago, Holland made waves with its position as "a tolerant place" for gay and lesbian visitors. At that time, the concept of "gay-tolerant" was a huge breakthrough, as Holland was among the first to explicitly work to increase gay visitor volume. Looking back, it is hard to imagine being "tolerated" by a destination, but it was a major achievement back then. Then came the "gay-friendly" approach. Several destinations arrived in the gay market in the late '1990s with their rainbow-hued advertisements to the GLBT community. The formula was in interpreting their mainstream creative to have gay appeal. It was a passive approach; better than "tolerant," but not quite an invitation. As social and political comfort levels increased in the early part of this decade, more ambitious marketing campaigns arose from a variety of destinations and travel services. They took the time to do gay and lesbian photo shoots, invested in clever ad and promotional campaigns, and worked within the community to identify best practices for internal organization and external outreach. The message became, "we are gay-welcoming" as

they rolled out the pink carpet for gay and lesbian travelers. The latest evolution phase of this important trend reflects an unprecedented global awareness of GLTB issues: The passing of marriage and civil union laws, increasing corporate equalization of employee benefits, and the appearance of gay characters in numerous TV shows and movies. The worldwide comfort level with our community is gaining momentum, and that is reflected in the increased comfort level in boardrooms as gay marketing is considered. Philadelphia, not even on the gay map only a few years ago, has led the latest competitive charge with a long-term, broad-based marketing campaign, which includes an award-winning gay-specific television ad. They are among a select collection of destinations that can claim to be "gay-aggressive." Montreal also made a breakthrough statement in its sexy ad campaign that stated, simply, "We love that you're totally out here." A far cry from "tolerant," Montreal actually loves us. These gay-aggressive destinations work within their local communities by forming "gay tourism advisory boards." They launch half-million dollar/year campaigns, track bottom-line results and present them in board meetings, and defend their position against negative politicians. They aggressively compete for our vacation dollars by aggressively competing for our attention with catchy ads and slogans. Air Canada, already a strong contender in the gay marketplace but now taking the step toward gay-aggressive, has been running a truly amazing ad that features the upward-pointing fuselage of a jet, with a small but suggestive message, "Enjoy the ride."

5. Single-image ads in a diverse market. This is where Community Marketing focus groups often become more animated and opinionated. Much of the advertisements that they see, much of what you spend thousands of ad agency dollars on, is not working. In some cases, we found that gay-market dedicated ads can actually be producing the opposite of your intended results for some people. Ad agencies like to be cutting edge. They like to present stylish and avant-garde creative concepts, to impress you and get the contract, and to win design awards. Unfortunately, that doesn't always translate to an effective campaign. Many ads we see coming into the gay market are "single image" ads, often featuring the stereotypical young white male. But the experiences that most operators and destinations offer are not one-dimensional, and the GLBT market is diverse. The ads that resonate best with most gay travelers depict a variety of people enjoying a variety of experiences. The gay community prides itself on its diversity

and inclusiveness. Ads that represent the GLBT community as young, white and male are poorly received, even among young, white males. Mainstream ad agencies are increasingly bringing mainstream clients to the gay market. This is great for everyone. But for an ad agency to assume that they can apply what they know about presenting a mainstream product or destination to a mainstream audience will apply to the GLBT market is to spend your limited gay market budget with little practical hope of success.

6. Gay + Diversity = Gayversity. Gayversity is simply an acknowledgement of diversity within the GLBT market. As more individuals become comfortable coming out, they bring with them their own individual interests, sensitivities, preferences and ideals. Bottom line? There is no "gay market." There are many gay markets, plural. CMI's research defines the story. With our enormous survey field of over 7500 participants, we have been able to delineate the similarities, as well as the subtle and not-so-subtle differences between segments within the GLBT market. Some of the destination trends and findings we identified include: Las Vegas is the #2 gay destination but not for any of the same reasons that other gay meccas have risen to the top. Chicago is a top destination among gay youth, who clearly prefer urban vacation experiences. Provincetown has wide international appeal, and has a particular strength among lesbian vacationers. Gay travelers of color have parallel destination interests and motivations as gay youth. As a case study, our research for Yukon Pride Adventures found that about half of gay and lesbian travelers surveyed nationally are very receptive to a Yukon-type of vacation. The other half are definitely not. The advantage to knowing who those 50 percent are is that it can help you focus your marketing budget, and maximizes your results. For example, does your destination or tour program appeal to gay and lesbian adventurers? Then join the Gay & Lesbian Sierrans, an activity section of the Sierra Club, attend their meetings, help with fund raising, join their board, and launch a direct marketing campaign to their membership. This is a grassroots way to make a difference, and earn loyalty. If you're clear on who your GLBT markets are (and ideally, you should be before investing in marketing), reaching out with a more personalized invitation directed to specific, appropriate GLBT market segments is what the future of "gay marketing" success will demand. Otherwise you are literally shooting your marketing budget into the dark.

7. The marketing power of inclusivity. "Inclusivity" is a word that does not exist. Exclusivity does, of course, but not

inclusivity. Here is the future of the GLBT market: Gays and lesbians 30 and under, and gay men and lesbians 60 and over are different animals. Community Marketing has learned this from research studies, as well as from qualitative focus groups throughout the USA and the UK. Younger gays and lesbians, obviously, foretell the trends of our market in the coming decade. Of course there are shades of gray, but this is the general delineation that Community Marketing is observing: Gays and lesbians age 30 and under are looking for messaging and imagery representing inclusivity. Your message to gay travelers 30 and under? Inclusive, diverse, integrated. "Gay" is no big deal. "Maybe I don't even identify with the word. Its just part of who I am; my straight friends have no issue. I have the confidence that I can go almost anywhere, stay in any hotel, and be who I am." Younger gay travelers don't have quite as much discretionary income, but by earning their loyalty now, you have the opportunity to create an annuity of business throughout their lifetimes. Generational differences are real. Different approaches to these markets are valid, and should be interpreted into your marketing plans.

8. The gay tipping point. Hotels are a case study in gay market-ing success, indicating a corporate tipping point in play. But not for the reasons you'd expect. There has been a significant shift in the hospitality industry over the last few years. "Gay-friendly" messaging was more important when relatively few hotels were positioning themselves as gay friendly. Just a few years ago, no major hotel groups or brands were found in the GLBT market. Sure, individual hotels were onboard in spe-cific markets. But not their parent companies or brands. At an HSMAI convention that I addressed in 1998, I made it clear that if a hotel company would take the leap into the gay market, they had a rare opportunity to become the "American Air-lines" of the hotel industry. Meaning that with a first-to-market advantage, they could claim an unshakable loyalty among gay travelers, similar to what American achieved by their historic entry into the market in 1993. But until just a few years ago, none of the major hotel brands heeded that call. Apparently, they all decided to jump in together though, because all of a sudden, most brands now appear in the gay media. The result is quite interesting, as identified in research. Because most hotels are now well represented in the gay media, gay consumers now assume that all hotels are gay-friendly. The exclusive use of gay messaging and imagery are no longer effective ways to move market share. In fact, practicalities are now the key motivators. The leading reasons that a hotel is

selected by gay and lesbian travelers now are that they have Internet access, are well-located, and have a restaurant and gym. Basic practicalities. It remains absolutely necessary for a hotel or brand communicate gay-friendliness, by noting their high HRC Index score, TAG Approved program participation, or IGLTA membership. Gay issues need to be included in sensitivity training. Hotels need to coach their front desk and concierge staff on gay issues and make them aware of local venues and events of interest to LGBT guests. But bottom line, now all that is simply expected. You need to bring "gay friendliness" to light, but in the larger context of the practical advantages of the property or chain. The historic transformation of the hospitality industry is a sign of things to come for other tourism segments, and the "gay market" as a whole. Don't sit on your gay-friendly laurels. To successfully earn or maintain market share, don't neglect to present the case for your product's or destination's practicalities of service, value, benefits and unique experiences.

And enjoy the ride we will, as more destinations, products and services make a difference within as they take the leap out.

Notes

1. Gay Tourism 2005, Greater Philadelphia Tourism Marketing Corporation, Community Marketing Inc.
2. Elderkin, Mark, International Gay and Lesbian Travel Association Convention, Speech, Washington, D.C., May 27, 2006.
3. Gray, Richard, Business Class, *Passport* magazine, November 2003.
4. Witeck, Robert, in-person interview, October 15, 2005.
5. Carrancho, Young, American Airlines, phone interview, November 3, 2006
6. Roth, Thomas, President and Founder, Community Marketing, Trends in Tourism 2006, Trends in Tourism 2007.

Appendix A: The commercial closet

Commercial Closet is a nonprofit that educates advertisers, ad agencies, academics, the media, and consumers for more effective and informed references to lesbian, gay, bisexual and transgender people in advertising, creating a more accepting place for GLBT people in society. The organization provides tools, years of reporting on approaches that have and haven't worked, research, consumer feedback and input from marketing, advertising, media and education leaders, and an online library with over 3000 global video and print GLBT-themed ad samples.

Michael Wilke[1] has charted the emergence of gay marketing and advertising since 1992. His work is widely cited by college textbooks and news agencies, and he is credited with coining the popular term "gay vague" by major newspapers.

Wilke is Executive Director and Founder of Commercial Closet Association, launched in New York City in May 2001. His syndicated column about gay marketing and media appears in leading gay newspapers and websites. He travels regularly across the United States and overseas with his video lecture, and consults to advertising agencies and corporations.

Wilke was a business reporter at *Advertising Age* for over four years and won a 1998 Gay & Lesbian Alliance Against Defamation (GLAAD) Media Award and was one of *OUT* magazine's OUT 100 in 2001 for his extensive coverage of gay advertising issues. In 2004 he was selected by *Girlfriends* magazine for its "Men We Love" issue. He has been an advertising judge for the ANA Multicultural Excellence Awards, a Crain Lecturer at Northwestern University's Medill School of Journalism, and in 2004 was awarded a Hearst Professional in Residence fellowship at the University of Colorado at Boulder. He has written about gay advertising and media for *The New York Times*, *Adweek*, *Brandweek*, *The Advocate*, Haymarket's *Revolution* marketing magazine and *Inside Media*. Wilke has appeared frequently on national news networks, internationally on CNN and the BBC, and on "Entertainment Tonight," "Extra!" and VH1 to discuss the subject.

Entering new media in 1999, Wilke became a news producer for New York City's WNBC-TV website, NewsChannel4.com, then helped launch CBSHealthwatch.com as a project director.

Wilke was a leader in the National Lesbian & Gay Journalists Association since 1992 and served as president of the organization's largest chapter, New York, from 1998 to 2000. He co-chaired the organization's 1998 national convention.

The Commercial Closet follows noteworthy gay-themed ads from major advertisers in gay publications and some relevant ones from mainstream media. For now, the bulk of the content in the archive is from two American magazines – *The Advocate* and *OUT*, with some representation by international titles, including Australia's *BLUE*, France's *Tetu*, the UK's *Gay Times, attitude* and *Diva*, and Belgium's *GUS*. *The Advocate* and *OUT*, formerly competing publications (founded in 1969 and 1992 respectively), were the premiere places for gay marketing for most advertisers through the end of the twentieth century. Print had long been the most developed medium to reach gay Americans, despite a handful of radio and local access cable programs.

Gay-themed print advertising has evolved parallel to the growing inclusion of gays in TV advertising in the United States. A substantial increase in gay-themed print ads began in 1996 as advertisers, particularly in the alcohol industry, sought to distinguish themselves in an increasingly crowded category. Alcohol and tobacco, both known as "sin" products, developed early because they were much less concerned about boycotts from religious conservatives than other corporate marketers.

Advertising spending in gay and lesbian publications reached $212 million in 2005 and $207 million in 2004, an increase of 28 percent over 2003, according to the 2005 edition of the Gay Press Report, the annual survey from *Rivendell Marketing* and *Prime Access*, which tracks 284 gay press publications. The 2004 report also found a jump in ads with "gay-specific" content through their copy or art direction, a jump of 241.9 percent over the previous year.

An additional $12 million is now spent annually in online advertising, for a total of $224 million in gay media alone. Another $8 million is spent on sponsorships of major national GLBT organizations and events, totaling $232 million spent on reaching the market.

Print ad revenues have quadrupled since 1994's $53 million and previously enjoyed consecutive double-digit gains annually: 1995 – 16.2 percent, 1996 – 19 percent, 1997 – 36.7 percent, 1998 – 20.2 percent, 1999 – 29 percent, 2000 – 36.3 percent.

However, the market remains like an Olympic-sized wading pool – very wide but very shallow because corporate spending and commitment remain low. As a result, research and understanding of the gay market remains poor. Detailed information is unavailable for gay media spending in other countries; however, the most developed markets outside the United States are Germany, Australia, England, Belgium and France. The nexus between marketers that include gays in their TV commercials and those that also have gay-specific print ads remains very small.

Lots of companies are already doing gay advertising. Over 1000 corporations and 500 ad agencies are represented in the Commercial Closet Ad Library, in categories such as alcohol/spirits, appliances, automotive, beauty, beverages, electronics, fashion, food, footwear, financial services, government, healthcare, media, package goods, restaurants, retail, soft drinks, telecommunications, travel and more. Specific data is difficult to come by, as companies rarely share proprietary information. But many marketers have repeatedly incorporated GLBT themes into mainstream commercials: Viacom (81), Unilever (31), IKEA International (22), Virgin Group (17), Levi Strauss & Co. (15), Volkswagen (14), Coca-Cola Co. (13), Heineken (9), Diesel (8), SABMiller (7), Orbitz (4), Polaroid Corp. (4), American Express Co. (4), Hyundai Corp. (3), John Hancock Financial Services (2), Visa International (2).

Gay-specific ad trends

For new companies entering the American gay market in 2003, more started off with gay-specific print ads rather than mainstream ads as they did in the past. Why do companies create gay-themed print advertising? They do it because even today there is so little imagery of gay men and women in ads that it stands out dramatically. And because the gay community so rarely sees itself reflected in advertising, those ads can get a disproportionately positive response if done properly. And of course an ad portraying the group it targets will usually do better than one that does not.

When polled about what types of ads corporations should run, the opinions of visitors to CommercialCloset.org varied. About 21 percent of 1000 polled said that ads should feature gay-specific pictures, while 17.9 percent thought mainstream ads would work – so long as they didn't picture heterosexual couples. But a majority, 52.8 percent, said that ads should be a mix of both.

Reflecting on the popularity of picturing shirtless men in gay men's magazine ads – particularly favored among fashion brands like Abercrombie & Fitch and Calvin Klein and beer advertisers like Miller Brewing Co. and Anheuser Busch – most Commercial-Closet.org visitors polled said they liked them, with 48.8 percent of 1500 respondents calling them "sexy/memorable." However, a large portion, 34 percent, also answered that such an approach was "predictable/boring," another 14 percent were neutral on the matter and 3.1 percent even found them "offensive."

The most developed ad categories targeting gay audiences include alcohol (140+ ads), fashion (140+), travel (50+), financial services (40+), automotive (35+) and media (35+), among others. Meanwhile, other categories remain largely missing, such as telecom, fast food, snack foods, packaged goods, electronics, personal products, household goods, healthcare, home, office, remodeling, retirement and many others.

While many companies have advertised for brief periods, a handful were in the market early and consistently keep a presence. They include V&S Vin & Sprit AB (the first major corporate brand in gay market initiated under Michel Roux in the United States but retain presence, Absolut vodka, 1981), American Airlines (1994), American Express Co. (1994), Anheuser-Busch Co. (1996 nationally), Diageo (all brands entered market pre-Diageo aquisitions in 1997 but retain their presence: Baileys – 1994, Captain Morgan – 1995, Chivas – 1995, Johnnie Walker – 1995, Jose Cuervo – 1996, Smirnoff – 1997, Tanqueray – 1995) IBM-1997, SAB Miller – 1994 (under Miller Brewing Co.), Subaru of America – 1996. Recent arrivals who have spent big or had a years-long presence and multimedia approach include Avis, Bridgestone, Ford Motor Co. (Volvo, Jaguar and Range Rover), Gruppo Campari (Skyy Vodka), Showtime Networks (for launches of Queer As Folk and The L Word). Among the most consistent gay-owned advertisers have been the cruise lines Olivia (for women), RSVP and Atlantis.

Commercial Closet Association Best Practices

Advertising seeks to sell, not offend. It may seem difficult today not to upset *someone*, but few minority groups are ridiculed as often and openly as gay, lesbian, bisexual and transgender (GLBT) people. We acknowledge that humor is an indispensable tool for creative professionals, yet while "political incorrectness" and irreverence may be assets to some in stand-up comedy, the goals of advertising are different – a laugh must also translate into sales from a wide variety of people. Over the years, hundreds of commercials have referred to GLBT people to spark attention and interest. Yet companies rarely consider what messages they may send inadvertently.

Although diversity and multicultural awareness are an increasing priority for corporations, and "sexual orientation" and "gender expression" concerns are addressed internally, these issues are often overlooked in general marketing communications. Advertising has not adapted to keep up with rapidly changing social attitudes of consumers, businesses, investors, employees, vendors and governments.

The general population and media are increasingly aware of diversity and uncomfortable with messages lacking sensitivity. At least 82 percent of Americans know someone gay, 81 percent of consumers don't care if products they regularly use are promoted to gays, 75 percent of youth support same-sex marriages, 54 percent of Americans support same-sex civil unions, and 42 percent of heterosexuals would be less likely to buy a product advertised on an anti-gay program. Viacom/MTV launched a 24-hour gay channel LOGO, primetime TV featured up to 30 gay characters, the U.S. Supreme Court confirmed gay protections, and same-sex couples have legal recognition in eight states, Canada, and 21 other countries. Big business increasingly protects its gay employees from discrimination (92.2 percent of *Fortune* 500), offers equal benefits (51 percent of Fortune 500), and explores gay marketing (36 percent of *Fortune* 100), with $235 million-plus invested annually in U.S. gay media, events and organizations.

Friends, family and colleagues of GLBT people are very vocal, active and sensitive allies to diversity issues, with national groups like PFLAG, GLSEN, and gay–straight alliances in schools.

GLBT people consistently self-identify in broad online surveys as 7 percent of the population (15 million-plus American adults). They belong to nearly every family and company, and hold $641 billion in buying power in 2006, growing annually. They vary in race, age, religion, national origin, gender expression, ability, politics, profession and class. About 1.2 million reported to the 2000 U.S. Census they are partnered in rural areas, suburbs and cities, appearing in 99 percent of counties nationwide, and 1 in 5 have children.

Advertising do's and don'ts

Effective advertising takes many creative forms, and is intended to inspire, motivate, persuade and educate audiences often in new and refreshing ways. Our "Do's and Don'ts" are not intended to be dictates but a useful tool to expand (rather than limit) creative thinking, and to enhance corporate messaging for all households and consumers, including GLBT individuals.

The information is based on professional trial and analysis from industry leaders.

To effect the most change within your business strategy,

- Do consider integrating GLBT people in general ad campaigns using tested business rationales such as diversity and welcoming all consumers. The simple power of inclusion works for many audiences.

- Do create GLBT-inclusive campaigns for both GLBT-media and general media whenever possible that are respectful to all.

- Do consider sponsoring and working with GLBT nonprofit organizations, if your company supports nonprofit causes. Sponsorships signal shared values, and can be helpful to understand GLBT sensibilities and community priorities.

- Do acknowledge that equal treatment of GLBT employees often is associated with companies practicing effective GLBT target marketing and GLBT-inclusive general marketing.

- Do understand the value of including openly GLBT participants in focus groups for all advertising reviews, when possible, regardless of target audience.

- Do provide expert GLBT awareness training on a regular basis for advertising and marketing staffs.

- Do understand that GLBT people are increasingly accepted by society and that insensitive messaging will be ineffective if not damaging.

- Do understand that few consumers will shun your brand for being GLBT friendly.

- Do recognize that GLBT people already are your customers.

- Do learn more about GLBT people, their demographics, media habits and brand preferences through qualified market research.

- Do understand it is important to test GLBT-themed ads, including those emphasizing masculine or feminine characteristics, with GLBT perspectives and in focus groups.

- Do consider offering GLBT marketing strategies when appropriately pursuing niche/multicultural/diversity marketing.

- Do tap into GLBT employee groups and retain GLBT marketing specialists/agencies/consultants for experienced guidance.

- Do coordinate GLBT marketing campaigns with general marketing campaigns.

- Do prepare consistent, business-like responses to media and consumer inquiries about GLBT-inclusive campaigns, focusing on business rationale, corporate values and the bottom line.

- Do identify the variety and number of business sectors creating GLBT-friendly marketing campaigns.

- Do understand that best practices toward GLBT inclusion begin at the top, with the endorsement and participation of senior executives.

- Do recognize that GLBT people come from all races, ages, ethnicities, nationalities, incomes, political and religious affiliations, professions, physical abilities and gender expressions, and whenever possible, incorporate such diversity into their representations. One size does not fit all.

- Do consider putting a twist on the old clichés of GLBT stereotypes, homophobia and transphobia.

- Do try to integrate GLBT characters as individuals and couples into "slice-of-life" and "everyday" depictions that reflect our diverse society.

- Do include real, openly GLBT celebrities, athletes and everyday people.

- Do choose inclusive and appropriate references to romantic relationships, families and individuals that are not exclusively hetero-centric.

- Do avoid using cliched and alienating GLBT stereotypes, homophobia and transphobia.

- Do consider including GLBT characters or real people without sensationalism.

- Do become aware of the differences between cross-dressers/transvestites, transsexuals, male-to-females, female-to-males, "bad drag," androgyny, and female impersonators/drag queens.

- Don't engage social conservatives in debate regarding GLBT issues, when criticized; business and respect for faith are separate issues.

- Don't waffle, modify or withdraw GLBT-friendly campaigns. Be consistent and principled.

- Don't avoid addressing missteps of legitimate GLBT concerns.

- Don't use GLBT stereotypes, themes or people as a device to elicit shock, humor or titillation.

- Don't use horrified or violent revulsion to references of homosexuality or transgender people.

- Don't label or degrade gay men or lesbians as sexual predators.

- Don't use sexuality in a degrading way to characterize same-sex affection and intimacy – or associate sexual practices with gays and lesbians differently than with heterosexuals.

- Don't characterize transgender people as deceptive, scary or freakish.

- Don't characterize bisexuals as cheaters.

- Don't create GLBT-sensitive messaging and imagery without testing independently with appropriate GLBT perspectives and/or focus groups

- Don't limit campaign feedback to one or two GLBT employees.

- Don't simply conclude that the average person will reject GLBT-friendly ads.

- Don't presume GLBT-friendly campaigns require disproportionately large budgets.

- Don't presume GLBT-friendly campaigns will be rejected by mainstream, national audiences.

- Don't use GLBT stereotypes without understanding the sensitivities and risks.

- Don't challenge the masculinity of men or femininity of women without understanding the sensitivities and risks.

- Don't use nonconformity to traditional gender roles for easy laughs.

- Don't marginalize and portray lesbians solely as straight-male fantasies.

Hundreds of companies and ad agencies represented in the Commercial Closet Ad Library have created GLBT-inclusive ads. They've done so to be edgy, to appeal to youth, for creative freshness and to reflect the diversity of their customers. Here are some suggestions for creative challenges. Gays and lesbians can be shown without relying on stereotypes or clichés. Try using

- Real gay or lesbian individuals. Authenticity goes a long way.

- Openly gay or lesbian celebrities or athletes.

- Same-sex pairings in everyday situations, such as at home, driving, shopping, eating.

- Same-sex pairings with physical affection.

- Sexuality can be referenced through verbal, text, graphical or anthropomorphic mentions.

- Unexpected twists, counter time-worn clichés and add other humor sources.

- A mix of masculine/feminine pairings for men or women as couples or friends: butch–femme (men or women), femme–femme (men), butch–butch (women).

Bisexuals are rarely shown at all, but when they are it is usually as duplicitous cheaters. How do you avoid that problem? Try using depictions without a defined relationship to another person and keep it ambiguous.

Transgender is an umbrella term covering a range of gender expressions, identities and situations: male-to-females/M2F, female-to-males/F2M, drag queens/camp, "bad drag," transsexuals, transvestites and androgyny. Trans people are not necessarily gay/lesbian. Most common in advertising are male-to-females, who typically show up as "deceptive" if they pass as women, or "frightening" if they do not. "Bad drag" and transvestites are intentionally unconvincing straight men half-dressed as women, for example wearing wigs and mustaches simultaneously, as a joke or with a mock-subversive motive like spying. Transvestites are depicted in ads as heterosexual men "caught" cross-dressing in women's undergarments. Drag queens are portrayed as campy men impersonating women. Transsexuals have had a sex-change operation. Female-to-males and androgyny – ambiguous gender – are rarely depicted in advertising. Why not try incorporating transgender people in everyday situations with acceptance as a twist, or employing camp/kitsch fun. Another option is to use a real transgender person or real female impersonator for authenticity.

Are stereotypes ever okay? It is often said that there is some truth to stereotypes, and indeed there are feminine/campy men, leathermen and masculine/sporty women, in the GLBT community. It would be exclusionary to say they should never be depicted. But remember, what is funny within a group of trusted friends or peers, or even in stand-up comedy, does not necessarily work for advertising. Such characterizations may be used with

173

caution if the intent is not to use GLBT stereotype for ridicule, and its presence works best as incidental or to ultimately counter a stereotype.

Note

1. Wilke, Mike, Founder and Executive Director, The Commercial Closet, www.commercialcloset.org, October 2006.

Appendix B: A list of GLBT organizations, meetings, conventions, sporting, religious and human rights groups

Below is a sample of the largest GLBT organizations, meetings, conventions and sport organizations. Check the Web for specific contact information as it may change often.

Aerospace Lambda Alliance

National Association of Lesbian and Gay Addiction Professionals (www.nalgap.org)

Association of Gay and Lesbian Psychologists (www.apa.org)

Black Gay and Lesbian Leadership Forum (www.nblglf.org)

Boeing Employees Association of Gay, Lesbians and Friends (www.noglstp.org)

Chevron Lesbian and Gay Employees

Coca-Cola Lesbian and Gay Employees

Dignity USA

Dupont (www.dupontbglad.com)

Ford Gay, Lesbian or Bisexual Employees (www.fordglobe.org)

Gay and Lesbian Alliance against Defamation

Gay and Lesbian Association of Choruses

Gay and Lesbian Athletics Association

Gay and Lesbian Medical Association

Gay, Lesbian, and Straight Education Network

IBM Employee Alliance for Gay, Lesbian, Bisexual, and Transgender Empowerment

Intel Gay, Lesbian, or Bisexual Employees

International Association of Gay Square Dance Clubs

International Association of Gay, Lesbian, Bisexual Jewish Organizations

International Association of Gay and Lesbian Judges

International Gay and Lesbian Aquatics

International Gay and Lesbian Law Association

International Gay and Lesbian Rodeo Association

Interpride

Lavender Law

Log Cabin Republicans

Microsoft Gay, Lesbian, Bisexual Transgender Group

National Association of Black and White Men Together

National Association of Gay and Lesbian Community Centers

National Gay and Lesbian Task Force

National Gay Pilot Association

National Gay and Lesbian Law Association

National Stonewall Democrats

North American Gay Amateur Athletic Alliance

North American Gay Volleyball Association

Out and Equal Workforce Advocates

Parents, Families, and Friends of Lesbians and Gays

Index